Meath

VOICES

Meath

VOICES

Tommy Murray

NONSUCH

Frontispiece: Saving the turf – Tullaghstown Bog.

First published 2006

Nonsuch Publishing
73 Lower Leeson Street
Dublin 2
Ireland
www.nonsuchireland.com

British Library Cataloguing in Publication Data.
A catalogue record for this book is available from the British Library.

ISBN 1 84588 524 4
ISBN-13 (from January 2007) 978 1 84588 524 3

Typesetting and origination by Tempus Publishing Limited.
Printed in Great Britain.

Contents

Acknowledgements

My sincere thanks to all whom have contributed in one way or another to this publication, especially to those that submitted stories or agreed to be interviewed:

Larry Daly, Brigid Smith, Andy Brennan, John Donohoe, Maureen Murray, Frank Murphy, Thomas O'Byrnes, Phyllis Gogarty, Janette Laffan, Kay Halligan, Tom Darby, Maedhbh Rogan, Myles Clare, Pat Farrelly, Mary Seery, Louise Scott, Mick Sheils, Tommy Grimes, Monica Sherlock, Frank Goodman, William G. Hodgins, Ann McEntee, Noel E French, Mary Jo Gibbons, Kathleen Rahill, Kathleen Miggin, Liam Smith, Paddy Duffy, Elizabeth Walsh Peavoy.

A special word of thanks is due to the four members of the Irish Wheelchair Association, John Darcy Dunderry, Bibi White Kentstown, Martin Faulkner and Kathleen Norris, both from Slane, for their contributions to this work.

========= ======== ========= ==========

My thanks is also due to those who supplied photographs: Eddie O'Brien, Harold Rayfus, John Magee, Thomas O'Byrne, Frank Murphy, Kay Halligan, Pat Farrelly, William G Hodgins, Anne Murray Browne, Tom Darby, Brendan Morley, Frank Goodman, Bill Lawlor, Tommy Grimes, Michael Sheils, Mary Seery, Maedhbh Rogan, Brendan Moynihan and Catherine Walsh.

Introduction

Following the success of my two most recent publications, *Trim – Looking Back* and *Voices of Trim* it seemed only logical that my next effort would take in the broader area of Meath. Time however, wasn't on my side as the rampant development of the county was obliterating all traces of the past. Villages such as Robinstown and Kilmessan were becoming towns. Places like Summerhill, Dunshauglin and Duleek were extending their boundaries weekly while Trim, Navan, Kells, Ashbourne and Athboy were seeing off some of the old buildings at an alarming rate.

In the case of Ashbourne the changes accelerated with every announcement. Here was a village of less than 400 souls suddenly finding itself with a population heading for 10,000. The once quiet village that's only claim to fame was a reported skirmish between Sinn Féin and the police in 1916, was now experiencing all the growing pains and publicity of an emerging metropolis. With the neighbouring villages of Dunshauglin and Rathoath also extending at an alarming rate it would seem that the foundation of a future conurbation in east Meath was in the making. Added to this was the stark fact that many of the people with real stories to tell were passing on, bringing their experiences with them.

Yet for all that I couldn't wait to get started. After all I had a fairly large private collection of old postcards and photographs of the county and, despite the fact that a number of them were already in the public domain, I felt certain that I would be able to get good quality images of Meath. As it happened, I did end up with close to one hundred images, accompanied by a lively prose.

Meath today means many things to many people. To some it means an All Ireland winning football team. To others it means the heritage sites like Newgrange, the Battle of the Boyne site or maybe the great castles at Trim, Dunsany, Slane or Killeen. Few can ignore the part played by the Boyne in the history of the county.

Situated as it is close to the capital and with an ever-increasing population, the environmental scene in Meath is one of constant change. The expansion in recent years of places like Navan, Trim, Kells Ashbourne, Rathoath, Dunshauglin, Dunboyne, Duleek and other centres has meant that hundreds of green fields have been lost to urbanisation. In some of the older towns whole streets have disappeared and in their place we have apartments blocks and shop fronts.

Back in 1906 the writer William Bulfin tells us that he was somewhat disappointed when his bicycle tour of Ireland took him into the heart of the royal county. He wrote of a county with huge hedgerows and copses stretching from town to town. Looking down at the county from the hill of Tara, he tells us that it was like a huge forest. It was the absence of people however, that made the greatest impression on him. It was just a lovely wilderness of grass, he wrote.

Today, over a century later, it is doubtful if Bulfin would recognise the county. The cattle tracks that he negotiated on his cycle from Ballivor to Tara have given way to busy roads fields have got bigger and the trees scarcer.

It is the pace of change in the last twenty years that has been the most noticeable. In Trim we used to gather blackberries around Newtown. Armed with three-quart cans we strolled at our leisure and picked the black and bronze harvest where today there are just front gardens and lawns.

While there have been huge developments in the larger centres it is more noticeable in places like Robinstown, where the village has more than doubled in size in the space of a few years.

It is a different kind of development however because in Robinstown it is fields that are being lost whereas it is the old and beautiful buildings that are disappearing in Navan, Trim and Kells. The thatched house and particularly the thatched pub are no longer a feature of the Meath scene.

The Beautiful Dean Swift Pub in Trim, Lawlor's Bakery Meal and Flour Store in Navan's Trimgate Street. Again in the same street The People's Café Hotel. Then where the structure may not have changed, the name over the door has, as is the case with Regan's pub beside Newtown Bridge. In the countryside the changes may be less noticeable unless of course it happens to be a large wood or area of wildflowers.

Take the case of Tobertynan Wood. Tobertynan Wood is just a few acres of woodland in a corner of Meath a few miles from the village of Rathmoylion. That it happened to be one of the most beautiful woodlands in Meath, if not the whole country, was something that was known to the people around the area. It contained some stately broadleaf trees and one particular skyscraper of a pine tree beneath which stood an altar to our Blessed Lady. At various times of the year, and particularly in the month of May, people came and prayed at the shrine and placed little bouquets of flowers at the base of the tree. Tobertynan was a place of tranquillity and beauty.

Every April and May still more people came to Tobertynan just to see the bluebells. For a few weeks every spring Tobertynan put on one of the greatest displays of bluebells imaginable.

Then in February 2000 the peace was shattered when a contractor moved in and without warning felled between fifty and one hundred of the biggest trees in the wood. Luckily the slaughter didn't go unnoticed and before a few hours had elapsed word spread and within a day or two it was actually discussed in the Dáil. What was left of the wood was saved but it was a close call.

How many more Tobertynans are there throughout the county? The number of trees being felled in the name of progress must run into thousands. A report in *The Meath Chronicle* as recently as December 2005 carried the headline 'Road Firm Could be Facing Fines of Up to Four Million Euro.' It went on to state that a road building contractor could be facing fines of up to four million euro for allegedly felling 157,000 trees to make way for the Trim Summerhill Road. According to the report the fine for illegally felling a tree is sixty-seven euro.

In Meath today the number of plants that are becoming victims of the urban sprawl is increasing all the time.

One plant however that is unlikely to become endangered is the Cow Parsley. It is a plant that seems to be more common throughout Meath than any other county in Ireland. Every year during the month of May, mile after mile of Meath roadside play host to this most prolific of plants.

Nor are the changes just physical, as traditions and customs that were once a way of life are now things of the past.

The disco has replaced the all night dance. First Communion and Confirmation, days that once brought whole communities to a halt, are now only noticed by those directly involved.

Even having a flutter with the bookies isn't what it used to be. Time was when a shilling, credit a shilling each way, reversed, was the standard bet and in the pub you would have the choice between porter and stout. Across the county from Dargan's pub in Longwood to the Cock McCabe's in Gormanstown a pint of porter was a shilling and a pint of stout was one shilling and three pence. That was in the early 1950s.

The Sunday game invariably involved such great football teams as Skryne, Navan O'Mahony's, Syddan, Drumbaragh and Kells Harps while Trim, Kilmessan, Longwood, Kildalkey and Killyon dominated the hurling scene on the Sabbath.

In the world of religion, the Corpus Christi procession and the parish mission still pack the streets and churches while the annual diocesan pilgrimage to Lourdes is as well supported as ever.

Tommy Murray
2006

About the Author

A native of Trim, Tommy Murray is better known as a poet. A winner of numerous awards for short stories and poems, his work has appeared both in Ireland and abroad. His poetry provided much of the background for the UTV documentary *Valley of the Kings* and was also featured on RTE's *Nationwide*.

As leader of the Meath VEC Adult Education Writer's Circle, he published five volumes of work as well as publishing eight books of his own. These include: *Memorable Meath Views, Something Beginning with Spring, Stella's Cottage, Where was Wellington Born, Once on Tara's Plain, The Boyne, Trim – Looking Back* and in 2005 Nonsuch published his highly successful *Voices of Trim*. During the early 1980s he contributed a regular column to *The Farmer's Journal* and *The Farmer's Monthly*. His stories appear regularly in *Ireland's Own*.

His awards for literature include The Gerald Manly Hopkins Certificate of Merit, The Patrick Kavanagh Memorial Certificate of Merit, The Nora Fahy Award, The Drogheda Mental Health Short Story First Prize, The Tom O'Shea Trophy in Swords in 2004. A runner-up in the Bard of Armagh contest in 2002, he was short-listed for the Strokestown Political Satire in 2002, 2004 and 2005. He also won The Poet of Fingall Competition in 2005 and 2006.

one

Voices of Meath

Over the years Meath voices have been raised on a variety of different subjects.

The Plain of Meath has none of the bleak monotony of the Connacht prairies.
William Bulfin.

Not for low born English hucksters, waileth our banshee.
Meath poet James Clarence Mangan in a reference to the fact that the banshee only followed the best bred Irish families.

Good night Ballivor I slept in Trim, two men and a man dead in Ballivor.
This senseless piece of prose originated among the gangs of workmen engaged in erecting stakes in the fields to prevent foreign aircraft from landing during the early 1940s.

He wouldn't hit a barn door with a banjo.
This is a uniquely Navan reference to those members of the FCA during the 1950s who were less that perfect marksmen on the rifle range.

Here too, stands, in the midst of one of the most wretched towns in Ireland, a pillar erected in honour of the Duke of Wellington.
One of William Makepeace Thackeray's less than complimentary observations during his visit to Trim in 1842.

If you can drink it or smoke it, it was for nothing, but once you have to eat it, it was dear.
Kells Shopkeeper Dave Butler commenting on the fact that people seem to complain about the price of everything except cigarettes and alcohol.

God, they'd give you an awful bite.
Comment from a local man while watching the lions being fed at Duffy's circus in Trim in the 1950s.

A wonderful town
British Labour leader Michael Foot during his visit to Trim in July 1991.

As long as you can see the sky between the leaves of the ash tree there's still time to plant potatoes.
Local Meath wisdom.

Moll Connor's house, Trim. A victim of the town's ever changing landscape.

Paddy Dempsey's cottage. A major contributor to the charm of the town.

If I ever have thoughts of making a figure in Ireland it will be at Laracor.
Dean Swift.

Trim indeed was never to become famous for industry but it has had a hand in shaping the lives of more than its share of world famous people.
Cyril Ellison.

Don't be too hard on yourself, your Honour.
Words of advice given to Mr Justice Beatty during a court case by a regular defendant in a drunk and disorderly case, who usually had his fine paid for by the judge himself.

It's well for you that you can afford to drink whiskey at 3/6 a glass.
Remark by the judge in a case where a Slane defendant was charged with being drunk and disorderly in a public place.

What I can't understand is how they managed to get the two of them in the one grave.
Meath solicitor Michael Regan responding to an inscription on local headstone which read, 'Here lies an honest man and a solicitor'.

He wouldn't hit a cow's arse with a shovel.
Overheard after a missed free during a hurling match in Kildalkey during the 1950s.

He wouldn't kick doors on a Halloween night
Comment about a certain Meath footballer after a less than inspiring game.

Apples, oranges and Peggy's leg that never wore a garter.
Catch cry of Athboy vendor Danny McGovern who sold sweets and fruit at football matches and other functions during the 1940s.

You see them in the distance and if they are moving they are crows but if they are not moving then they are probably council workers.
Meath county councillor referring to members of the outdoor staff in the 1950s.

two

Landmarks

A Well Loved Statue

Elizabeth Hickey died in 1999 and I had the privilege of being asked to write a poem to her memory by her family. It was indeed with not a little pride and sadness that I listened to that poem being read at her funeral service in St Mary's Protestant Church, Navan.

During her lifetime Elizabeth wrote a number of excellent books and without exception I would be the first to get a signed copy of each of these books. Over the years we discussed literature and history and on more that one occasion, the interior of Skryne Castle itself. She told me of her efforts to save the statue of St Patrick on the Hill of Tara. Here is what she had to say on that subject.

A familiar and well-loved figure is still missing from Tara. On the morning of 26 June the statue of St Patrick was removed from its site on the summit of the hill and relegated to the yard of the Office of Public Works in Newtown.

This caused much sorrow; both among local people and among visitors from further afield. The statue was not a masterpiece and its artistic merit has been much disclaimed among the cognoscenti. This does not matter. It was a kindly representation of Ireland's national saint carved by a Navan man, William Curry, and erected at his own expense at the end of the nineteenth century. Artistically it symbolised an Ireland by way of finding its own values again. An Ireland perhaps, of shamrocks and wolf hounds, of round towers and mitred saints; but a more serious Ireland also of scholars such as Douglas Hyde and Eoghan O'Growney, and of idealists such as Horace Plunkett. The political Ireland of Charles Stewart Parnell. There were many strands to that Ireland and William Curry's statue was but one.

A similar statue was placed on the summit of Croagh Patrick to symbolise the banishment of the snakes from Ireland. St Patrick on Tara symbolised the saint's contention with the overthrow of the pagan druids and beginning of his Christian mission to the Irish. Neither of these contentions may be strictly true; what matter, the symbol is the important fact: childish perhaps to write thus but Saint Patrick on Tara entered many a childish mind and remained to influence many an adult man and woman.

A committee was formed by Rathfeigh Historical Society to petition the Office of Public Works to restore the statue of Saint Patrick to Tara. Anyone who feels strongly on this matter should contact the Secretary, Rathfeigh, Tara, County Meath.

Elizabeth Hickey had strong views on history and especially the history of Meath. In the opening lines of her wonderful little book 'The Legend of Tara' she has this to say.

Some places on this old earth on which we dwell seem always to have had a history and Tara is one of these places. It is not vastly impressive today but from the most ancient times it has held a place in the hearts of Irishmen unequalled and unique.

King John's Castle, Trim. The gate and wall have long since gone.

The Hill of Slane, an important landmark in the county's heritage.

It stands for ancient splendours and legendary deeds, for memories of kings and champions and early Christian saints, for battles with the Danes and the '41 rebellion; for the men of '98 and the Great Emancipator. Indeed to write adequately the story of Tara would be to write much of the history of Ireland and the history of Ireland is one of the longest histories in the world.

Time has shown however that Elizabeth Hickey did go on to write the history of Tara in what can only be described as the most concise and condensed account of life on the famous hill.

Going Down to the Caves

Elizabeth Peavoy is a published poet and writer in her own right. A daughter of internationally acclaimed writer Mary Lavin, Elizabeth here describes some aspects of growing up in Bective.

The caves were a great attraction for visitors to the country for a day away from the city. It was also a spot of local history and lore. The beehive mounds were meant to have served as a hideout in the days of the Croppy boys but were actually said to be used as a grain store. On our knees we crawled through the leaf mould and bramble that led to the opening chamber of the first cave. It was said that they were used as a hideout for monks, transferring gold vessels back and forth to the Abbey, during the raids by Cromwell on the Cistercian Monastery of Bective. The caves were also meant to be a continuation of a lengthier passage across the river, and we tapped the walls hoping to be the one to find a secret enclave going nowhere. Whatever their purpose, the caves were a major attraction and source of awe for the locals and the visitors.

'Going down the caves' was a very pleasant way to spend the afternoon when the visitors from the city were beginning to pall and we wanted to enliven the day or maybe dazzle them by our daring. 'Have you got a candle or matches?' It was stipulated that in order to be sure of the amount of oxygen in the cave a lighted candle would provide a safe passage into the innermost chamber, of which there were two. If the candle extinguished itself, it meant instant loss of life and hope. The candle, once lit and held preciously by the bearer, into and under the weeping walls, never failed to light the way ahead into a passage. There was also a fear that a fox might have been sheltering within and thus disturbed might have overpowered us. These ideas however were fanciful and nothing occurred to uproot or startle us when we were intruding on the wildlife, a belief that is still true where the pheasants have taken over the Bective woods.

Along the Claddy were the remains of an old churchyard, which was overgrown and sometimes flooded. Across Bective Avenue led to an embankment of silted gravel, in which a mass grave was uncovered. My mother decided the graves were worth investigation and spoke of getting a man from the museum to classify them and the mass burial. Finding bones of animals was not unusual in the Abbey precincts, although this was an unusually large find of human remains and skeletons in the peaceful grazing land. For days we spoke about the outcome of an exhumation of skeletons and amazed ourselves by visions of this dance with death. I don't think the man came from the museum, although I'm certain that a great deal was spoken of the cause and effect of this unceremonious burial in unsanctified ground. I think it was suggested in the end that the shallow tomb might have been the result of the famine, which was inside the Boulton Estate of Bective where times were not quite as bad as they had been 'West of the Shannon.'

Then a couple of years later when oil appeared in the kitchen taps with no apparent explanation, there was an idea that we would have to drill for oil. It was at the time of the exploration of oil in the vicinity of Navan and location of minerals at Tara and then Bula gave rise to certain expectations. Yet nothing could be allowed to disturb the peace of the area around the Abbey, a national monument, Crossen's cottage sand, the preserved fishing along the River Boyne, not even a hiker straying off the beaten track onto the back road between Bective and Athboy.

Another idea of my mother's was that we should never bend to drink water directly from the tap, in case of frogs or beetles coming up from the well. The air locks, as the rattle in the pipes was called, did not denote foreign bodies but preserved the notion that what we found in the bath were from the large community of insects ready to encroach on our lives and we might have to suffer the fate of Little Ada. We did put our heads under the pump to quench thirst having walked the roads from Bective to Kilmessan when we won the sports and had to walk home again empty handed. There was a spirit of rivalry, that preserved the spirit of local communities which kept them apart by somehow being better.

Local interest was once again aroused when the film *Captain Lightfoot* was shot at the Abbey, starring Rock Hudson's many doubles. Again the making of *Braveheart* aroused local passions for movie stars never before encountered. Yet we did our best to invigorate and respond to the myth and history in the making during those forays in the Bective woods. Each place was described by name, the Abbey Field, the Round Wood, and the Railway Wood, the Style Field, Mitchell's Field for mushroom picking and Bective Avenue for collecting sprigs.

A great love for the countryside and fields of Meath was characteristic of a woman such as she was, Mary Lavin, my mother. It was a carryover from her childhood in New England where she grew up along the banks of the Neponset River. I was later to learn that the characteristic shrub of that region is lilac. Perhaps that is one reason why one of her early stories was called *Lilacs*.

That story is about a dung heap. The theme running through it is that side by side with the reality of the Carter collecting and dealing in manure for his livelihood it is a tale of promise and disappointment and the energy of regeneration and renewal. It is an inflatable dream and yet can be a magnate for the sordid view of things at the bottom.

There was not much dung around Bective alongside the river and the trees and the horses. The old forge was a parcel of folklore, but that has long since been bulldozed. Maybe the Ceide fields could have been situated in Meath pastureland rather than in Mayo. Strange to hear the big road to bring power and access to the small townlands will mean some of this hinterland will disturb links with the past.

Elizabeth Peavoy Walsh

Oldcastle Church

I was born in Oldcastle and I still live here, in Spring Hall to be exact. I am a member of the local Catholic community. St Brigid's, that is the name of the parish where I go to mass, has two churches, the church of St Oliver being the main church. The other church in the parish, Moylough, is about three miles distant and is smaller.

A stunning view of Slane Castle as it appeared in 1907.

Battle of the Boyne site between Slane and Drogheda.

King William's Glen, a strategic site during the Battle of the Boyne.

THE WEIRS, NAVAN.   PUB. BY MEATH CHRONICAL LTD.

This weir at Navan is one of many along the river Boyne.

My brother, Father Patrick Rahill, is in America. I am a member of the Legion of Mary and I like to play a part in all the parish activities. The Parish Priest here is Father Conlon and the curate is Father O'Brien. As far as I know the church was built in 1905 and the spire wasn't added until much later, sometime around the 1930s I think.

We have a special mass every year on 1 July in honour of St Oliver who was born in Oldcastle. In the grounds outside there is a plaque stating where the President Mary McAleese planted a tree on the occasion of the celebration of St Brigid's Church on 16 May 2004.

The Parochial House is nearby and while I am not sure how long it has been built I feel sure that it is even older than the church. There was also a church hall with a reading room and billiard tables, but that is long since gone and there is a house now in its place.

We have two masses on Sunday and of course the vigil mass on Saturday evening and we also have the most wonderful choir under the leadership of Chrissie Gogarty.

A relic of the saint is housed in a glass case on the altar and visitors come to see it regularly as a result of this many coffee chops have sprung up around the area.

Kathleen Rahill

St Joseph's Convent of Mercy, Navan.

I have to be completely honest when I say that the decision to include this little history of St Joseph's Convent of Mercy, Navan in this book was greatly influenced by the fact that I had some rare and wonderful pictures of the building. These were not just ordinary pictures like so many that we see in banks and other public buildings.

The two pictures, which depict the 'Grotto' and the 'Community Room' actually came from two postcards published as far back as 1918, were extremely rare and were posted in Navan on the 14 July of that year.

Finding someone to write the piece didn't present a problem because I already knew that Noel French had done something in his own book on Navan. While the actual views will hardly stir any memories, I do hope that they will add something to the history of St Joseph's. Always knowledgeable on anything to do with the history of Meath, here is Noel's contribution to the publication of the pictures.

In 1853 a group of nuns from Kells arrived in Navan and settled in a house in Academy Street, which Fr. Eugene O'Reilly had bequeathed to them. The Sisters of Mercy opened a sewing school in Bakery Lane with funds provided by the Duke of Bedford, who was the local landlord.

The Mercy National School was taken under the Board of Education on the 1 June 1856. One year later the order took over Leighsbrook House. Leighbrook was described as a gentleman's house in the Ordnance Survey namebooks in 1836. The area had been the site of the chapel of Navan for a period of about seventy years in the previous century. The Sisters raised the roof of Leighbrook House and constructed a school there. The school provided education for boys and girls right up to sixth class. A new primary school was erected in 1910.

St. Joseph's registered as a secondary school in 1925. Many of the students of the secondary school entered the teacher training colleges or university or went to work in the civil service. It provided education to boarders and day pupils and the curriculum included such vocational subjects as typewriting and domestic economy. A new secondary school was erected in 1968-71 and extensions were added in 1975 and 1982.

Noel E. French

Stories to Tell

'Meath is a county steeped in history. Despite the ravages of time and the frequent destruction of its monasteries and friaries by invading armies it remains to this day one of the most interesting counties in Ireland. Within its boundaries are contained numerous ancient crosses, fortresses and extensive and picturesque ruins.'

Tommy Murray, *Memorable Meath Views*, 1989.

When it comes to landmarks and particularly historic ones, Meath is probably better endowed than most counties. Some like the Hill Of Tara and Newgrange are known throughout the world.

'The Hill of Tara beautifully bears witness to the epic adventures of Ireland's royal past, to the battles and celebrations of the High Kings.'

Meath Tourism Brochure.

While some of the landmarks such as St Joseph's Convent of Mercy or the Old Forge in Navan have long since ceased to exist, the Hill of Tara continues to draw the visitors in their thousands.

'Few districts in the kingdom can show so much lovely scenery, and into no part of it are compressed so many ancient sites, ruined castles, fine old churches and abbeys and famous battlefields as that stretch of country drained by the Boyne and the Blackwater.'

Richard Lovett, *Ireland 100 Years Ago.*

Today these ancient monuments and landmarks speak to us across the centuries. They all have stories to tell. Even those as obscure as the thatched cottage or the redundant railway bridge have a story to tell.

The Changing Face of Meath

My aunt kept a revolver in the drawer, an old rusty model from the troubles. When I enquired whether it worked she replied 'Nah, but I'm thinking of getting it fixed, just in case.' In case of what I never asked, but the stories were told and the door was open. On my mother's side her uncle could regale with equal alacrity. What they had in common was a generation that paid scant regard to authority.

The area I grew up in was never short of such characters. Whether more or less than any other area I don't know, but it is difficult to put a finger on what actually defines a character or indeed a place, whether it's the people or does the place itself

River, bridge and ancient ruin at Newtown Trim.

Horseshoe Weir in the Boyne Valley.

lend something. People or place, the small villages around Tara have been to the fore in this part of county Meath for over a hundred years, and you don't get to be different by being the same.

The Hill of Tara was the seat of High Kings for centuries and lists of associations are too numerous to mention. It was the centre of a civilisation that existed in some form until the coming of the Normans and was itself part of that complex that includes Newgrange, Knowth, Dowth and the Hill of Ward etc.. Burial mound or forts I don't know, but to describe the people who built them as having an interest in astronomy is an understatement.

But it is not just the area around Tara; most of the county is steeped in history, from the Megalithic Burial Mounds to Great Houses and Norman Castles to Monastic Sites and more. It is a heritage that should be protected.

Today, except in a historical or sporting sense, there is no centre to this region, places that have historical significance are being gradually sucked into the greater Dublin area. A vast urban sprawl of housing estates, satellite towns and motorways that run from one roundabout to the next where sameness is the norm.

In recent years this region of County Meath has enjoyed great economic success but it is difficult to see this except in terms of personal wealth. There are no great hospitals; few public works while utility buildings dot the landscape. Indeed in this region the hospitals have been downgraded and the railways pulled up.

The towns of County Meath, like the towns of every other county, have become unfriendly places, curfew hours, places where you buy time from a machine, places to get out of rather than go into, shop and go, part of the great commuter belt, houses built on smaller plots of land, a lesson not yet learned.

Frank Murphy

The County Home

My earliest recollection of St Joseph's Hospital, or the County Home as it was then called, are of seeing the handcart being pushed from the building down the hill to the cemetery at the Maudlins. Trotting alongside to school we weren't aware then that this was actually a burial ceremony that was being enacted. It was something that happened on two or three mornings every week, and more if there was a flu epidemic in the area. This was back in the 1940s long before the route was bisected by the town's inner relief road. Looking back now I suppose we should have wondered about the scene but we just didn't even give it a second thought. If indeed we had an inkling as to the nature of these little excursions we would have at least crossed ourselves. One can only guess how many souls made their last journey inn these handcarts.

Many years later I was to work in the County Home as assistant gardener to John Fedigan. It was during this period that I learned that the county home was a law onto itself. For one thing it was self sufficient in the provision of not only vegetables but bacon too.

Among the many jobs that I had to do was the cutting of as many as thirty heads of cabbage on three mornings every week and delivering them to the kitchen. The County Home was self-proficient in the provision of bacon to go with the cabbage

A tranquil river Boyne at Navan.

Beauparc House in the Boyne Valley.

as anyone living within a mile or so of the place could verify. The whole town knew when they were killing pigs in the county home. The squealing would go on for an hour. Who actually did the killing I don't know but I suspect that one of the local butchers would be called in to do the necessary.

The relationship between the inmates, particularly the men, and the people of the town was one of mutual respect. Easily recognisable with their rough homespun cloths, many of these men were well known characters. This was a time when there was a certain respect for the elderly and many of these men were known by their Christian names, and so we had Ned and Phil among others. They were nothing if not individualists and they all had their little idiosyncrasies. One in particular had the habit of kicking every paper bag he came across on the street. Nothing wrong with that until a certain joker decides to put a brick in one of the paper bags in his path, resulting in great discomfort to the kicker.

Another walked with a distinguishable slouch while yet another was a familiar sight as he went about his morning and evening round delivering newspapers.

One of the most popular inmates of the County Home ever to grace the streets of the town was actually deaf and dumb, yet his personality was such that he stole the hearts of all who knew him.

Tommy Murray

The Old Forge at Corn Market Navan

Having recently published a book about his young days growing up in the town of Navan, Mick 'the Sheriff' Sheils has suddenly come into the limelight as a local historian of some standing. Here Michael gives us a first hand account of the old forge in Navan's Corn Market

When I was a young boy growing up in Navan, there used to be an old forge at Corn Market in the centre of the town. It was worked by John Curtis, 'Gussie' and although it was a time of great decline in the blacksmith industry, Gussie was kept busy and I was privileged to witness a master at work. Many times on my way home from school I stopped for a while to watch Gussie shoe a horse.

The forge had a chimney, a fireplace and an anvil. There was a large bellows beside the fire with an overhanging handle attached. One had to pull hard on the handle to generate enough heat to render the iron pliable so that the blacksmith could work it into whatever shape he required. Customers often took turns at pumping the bellows while Gussie banged and shaped the iron with a heavy hammer.

A special type of coal called slack was used for forge work. Unlike domestic coal which came in lumps slack came in granules. Gussie mixed water with the slack before putting it in the fire as it gave better results that way.

The iron for the horseshoes came in long bars. Gussie would cut a piece from one of the long bars and place it in the fire. Then he would pump the bellows to make the fire stronger until the iron glowed at which point he would remove it from the fire with a long pincers and hammer it into shape while it was still glowing red. I loved the ringing clinging sounds he made as he worked the iron on the anvil. When the shoe was near the correct shape he inserted a file into a nail hole on the outside of the shoe to hold the hot shoe in place. I can still hear the sizzling sound and smell the smoke as the shoe burned into place. When the shoe was exactly the right shape Gussie would put it into the trough of water to cool it down. He would continue working the same way until all four shoes were made. Then he would select some nails and hammer the shoe to the hoof. Oh, how my teeth cringed the first time I saw him drive the nails home.

Gussie wore a special apron made of leather. It had a slit in the centre, which went to above his knees; this enabled him to hold the horse's hoof between his knees while he fitted the shoe.

Most animals were quiet during the shoeing process. Flighty ones could be a problem and Gussie relied on the help of the owners to keep them under control. Sometimes an owner would lose the battle with a jittery beast. When this happened Gussie used a special implement called a 'touch.' A touch was a long stick with a small loop of rope fitted on the end. Gussie didn't like to have to use the touch but it was necessary on occasion. He would simply pull down the touch and give it a twist. This controlled the horse until the shoe was fitted.

Sometimes an animal would be brought in with loose shoes, which weren't well worn. These were called slippers and the blacksmith didn't need to make new ones. Instead, he would remove the old ones, reshape them and nail them on again. Fitting slippers on took less time and cost less than new ones.

As well as the noble art of horse-shoeing that has faded into the mists of time, Gussie did general repair work to ploughs, harrows, mowers, reapers, etc.

Gussie was also a Weight Master. There was a small weigh-bridge in Corn Market just outside the forge which he used for weighing small loads and there was a much larger one on Circular Road for lorries. I can remember standing on the weigh-bridge at Circular Road with groups of other children to feel it vibrate under our feet.

The forge was sited in an old stable which was used to keep horses overnight when hay and straw and other general produce were transported by horse and cart to Dublin.

Gussie worked the forge from the year 1936 until 1978 when he retired. After the forge closed down John Smyth, who has a very popular pub in Academy Street, Navan, bought all the equipment originally used in the forge. John turned part of his premises into a museum depicting the old forge and all the original equipment is now on display in the reconstructed version.

The bellows itself dates back to 1870 when Hyland's Coach Works, Fair Green and Navan used it. It was later transferred to Hyland's Coach Builders in Trim Gate Street in 1910. Hyland's closed their coach building business in 1929 and sold the same bellows to John Curtis. Gussie worked it until he retired and it is still in perfect working order thanks to John Smyth.

Visitors to the town of Navan and especially those with a sense of history would be pleasantly surprised by a visit to Smyth's pub, which is situated, beside the railway viaduct. There they can have a meal and quench their thirst in pleasant surroundings and witness part of Navan's history at the same time.

An exact image of the forge has been recreated by local artist Patrick (Patsy) Reel, in 1972. It can be seen in the greater bar area where it generates the atmosphere and the era in which it flourished as a working and a meeting place for coachmen and farmers alike and will almost certainly capture the imagination of today's visitor.

Michael Sheils

Killeen Castle in 1920.

A castle in its own right but many of these Parnell cottages have been altered beyond recognition..

The picture reproduced here is from an old postcard of Duleek in 1913. The postcard was sent from Duleek to an address in England. From the writing, we learn that the weather in Duleek on 10 September 1913 was sunny.

This is how Duleek would have been appeared to a visitor in 1910. It was here in the fifth century that St Patrick erected the first stone and mortar church built in Ireland.

The People's Park

Brigid Smith is a literacy tutor who has been writing on and off for years. She runs a successful bar in John Street Kells and her knowledge of the local history is reflected in the following observations.

As one travels along the Oldcastle Road from the town of Kells, approximately one mile from the town itself on the right hand side is a beautiful park known as The People's Park. This park was renamed in recent years and as one enters it there is a long paved path leading from the roadway up to the top of the hill where the Spire or Tower of Lloyd stands. To a stranger this is a fabulous facility for children and indeed the adults of the town to come and enjoy the fresh air and beautiful scenery.

There is a beautiful children's play area with swings and slides and wooden picnic tables all around the grassland. On a summer's day the park is alive with fun and games and little children can be heard playing and laughing and enjoying the facilities.

The tower itself stands stately and tall at the pinnacle of the hill and from there one can see for miles around the plains of Meath and surrounding counties. In the distance the sweeping valleys and rolling hills and faraway busy roads the traffic appears like a swarm of busy bees and insects toiling away. This is a spectacular sight for any eyes to behold and well worth a trip on a clear day.

However, when one looks more closely into the history of the park it is indeed a much more depressing picture as this was in earlier time known as Pauper's Graveyard. To the north of the tower, which was built in 1791 by the First Marquis of Headfort called Taylor to commemorate his father, stands a large old Celtic type tombstone. It bears the stark inscription 'Erected to the memory of the poor interred here during the operation of the English Poor Law System 1828-1921 R.I.P.' As one stands there and ponders, one can get images of poor starving corpses having died from cholera or fever being buried here. How miserable and hungry and sickly they must have been. These people would not have had a decent burial as we know it, but instead may be buried in twos or more in an open grave without the benefit of a coffin.

It is said that in famine times, corpses taken from the Dead House at the back of the Workhouse were transported here for burial instead of having to be brought down the town from the Moynalty road where the Workhouse was situated en route to St John's cemetery, on the opposite end of the town near the Navan Road. The reason for this was that it could be done discreetly in order not to scare the residents of the town.

At that time there would have been no proper roads, only dirt passages and one can visualise two or three lean corpses thrown on the back of a horse-drawn or hand pushed cart and transported here to their final resting place.

The graveyard dates from 1851 and evidence from the minute book of Kells Workhouse shows a resolution establishing this burial site dated 16 February 1850 which reads:

'The Poor Law Guardians to make or cause to be made a lane or passage from the dead house at the rear of the workhouse to the road leading to Lloyd, so as to prevent the corpses intended for internment to be paraded around to the front of the workhouse to the danger of the inmates and guardians, or through the town which would affright and endanger the inhabitants'.

The workhouse was established in 1841 on a site near Mabes Bridge on the Moynalty Road. It was a grey stone building rather like the workhouse of the day. It ceased to function in 1924 soon after the abolition of the Poor Law System and the formation of the Irish Free State.

This particular site was, under the circumstances the most conveniently located one suitable for the above purposes.

There is a stone wall around the grounds of the tower in which is situated a stone altar which would remind one of a mass rock and one can visualise a priest on the run in Penal times, trying to celebrate mass here. It gives the feeling of sanctity and remorse. In front of the stone altar there is a huge boulder or slab of stone, on which the inscription reads, 'In the immediate aftermath of the great famine this mass burial place was opened in 1851 for the poor people of Kells District. Their memory challenges us to end the scandal of hunger in today's world of plenty. Erected by a FRI Great Famine Project 9/10/93.'

This inscription would indeed make one wonder, in today's world of full and plenty, how any nation would have to endure such hardship and hunger, when one hears of mountains of food being held in storage all over the world.

This is only one of many beautiful and stark reminders of times gone by. Indeed one would need about a week in Kells in order to explore the many great historical and religious reminders of famine times in this part of County Meath.

Brigid Smith

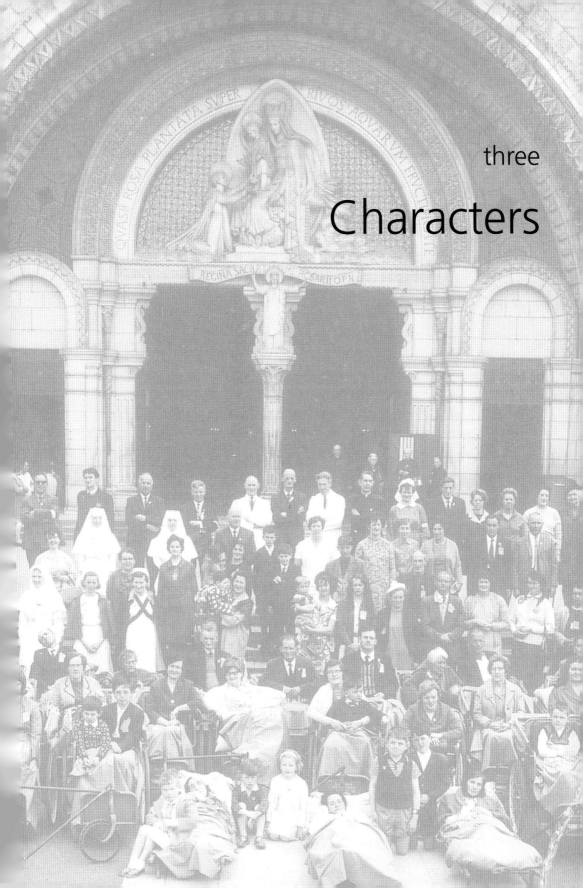

three

Characters

Andy Brennan Remembers

During the 1950s the FCA was a way of life for more than a few Meath men. During those years members of the part time force were involved in nearly every function of any importance that took place in every part of the county. Whether it be parading or providing a guard of honour for the Corpus Christi processions or making a name for themselves on the rifle range they were seldom out of the news.

Today fifty years on many of these men are still with us, hale and hearty and all with stories to tell. One such man is Andy Brennan from Navan.

Until I met Andy Brennan I never realised just how committed a part time soldier could be to his calling. Andy was the deputy Mayor of Navan when I spoke with him in the Navan library on 14 January 2006. Here is his story.

I joined the FCA on 7 March 1950 and twenty-five years later to the day I received my honourable discharge. This period of service entitled me to two medals. For completing twelve years service I received The Distinguished Service Medal with one bar and for completing twenty-one years service I received the Distinguished Service Medal with two bars.

It is surely a measure of Andy's fondness for the FCA that he can still remember his army number.

Indeed I can, it is 613722.

How were you on the targets?

Well according to the officers in charge they put me down as an exceptional and consistent marksman.

I was a member of the South Meath Platoon that came third to the Pierce and 26th Battalion in the early 1950s. The FCA in Meath was at its height then and I can still recall many of the other members of that battalion. There was the McGoonas, Paddy and Jimmy from Navan, Tim Higgins from Longwood, Lt. John Clarke from Duleek, Jack McGlew, Cpl. Cullen from Dunshaughlin, Benzer Byrne from Longwood, Tommy Murray from Trim, Dessie Farnan from Trim, Leo Byrne from Navan, Billy Connell from Connells's Cross, C S Michael Brady and of course Christy Stapelton. These are just a few that immediately spring to mind.

I spent my summers in camp and I would either go the Cork, Kilkenny or Gormanstown although my fondest memories are of the County Meath camp. I remember once when I was doing butt duty. This was where we would have to signal back to the marksmen just how they had scored. In the initial stages the riflemen would be expected to get a four inch eight inch or twelve-inch group. Getting the bullets into a four-inch grouping would be the ultimate aim. Then there were soldiers that

Regan's Pub beside St Peter's Bridge at Newtown, Trim. The name over the door has since been changed..

The beautiful Dean Swift Pub in Trim has been replaced by a more modern establishment.

just couldn't get anywhere near a grouping and when one of them asked me one day how did he do 'Did I get a four,?' he asked. I replied, 'Definitely you did get a four, a four footer.

I competed in all the competitions including The Walsh Cup which was a competition open to all the centres and Navan won it but I was runner up in the individual placing.

Then there was the Gordon Darker Cup for hand grenade throwing and this was something that I was well practised at and it was no surprise when I won that cup.

Life in Gormanstown camp at that time was not without a certain amount of humour and I remember one day when we were lining up for breakfast. The usual breakfast was a quarter of a loaf and a small amount of butter. Then someone asked one of the soldiers, Oliver McDonnell, what was the stain on his knife obviously thinking that the knife hadn't been washed. You can imagine the surprise on the officer's face when Oliver said that it wasn't a stain, it was his butter ration.

One of the most unforgettable memories I have of the annual camp was the time when a group of us were doing guard duty. Sometime after midnight we heard footsteps and challenged with the usual Halt Who Goes There? This was repeated three times with no response.

So we fired and the next morning all hell broke loose when it was discovered that we had killed a donkey that had strayed from a local traveller's encampment.

Interview with Andy Brennan on 14 January 2006

Granddad

My grandfather was a building contractor and joiner (a much more lucrative business, if he were around today!) He worked from his workshop adjacent to the family home, as well as building houses and other construction work in different parts of the county. During the thirties and forties the Health Board gave him contracts to build farm labourer's cottages around Meath, many of which stand today as quaint and as picturesque as ever.

One of granddad's favourite places in Meath was Slane and its surrounding area. On a Sunday drive he often took his three daughters, Patricia (my mother), Gertie and Carmel, there. Granny, of course, insisted on staying at home to say the rosary before they'd even closed the doors of the old Ford car. As a young man, one of granddad's contemporaries and acquaintances was the poet Francis Ledwidge, they happened by one another from time to time, and while during the course of conversation they might never have discussed poetry in any great depth or Frank's own works, granddad always enjoyed their encounters and was saddened at his untimely death in 1917, little knowing at that time the extent of Ledwidge's literary ability.

Another one of his acquaintances was the venerated Matt Talbot, whom he met during the early 1920s when he bought timber from the wholesaler's T&C Martin and Brooke Thomas, Dublin. In one of these timber yards, Matt Talbot's duties as a yardman was to help load the lorries, vans and trailers. It was while attending to this task that granddad made his acquaintance. Although thirty years his junior my grandfather was nonetheless struck by Matt Talbot's strength of character, his sunny disposition and willingness to help others. He said, 'to have met Matt Talbot was to have met an exceptional individual.' Some fifty years later in 1975 the church decided that from a human point of view the same man had the qualifications of a saint.

Occasionally granddad would be commissioned to make confessional boxes for various parishes in the county, two of which are still very accommodating in St Mary's Church, Navan.

One day while granddad was about to hand carve one such confessional box, my mother remembers as a young child running in and out of it with her two younger sisters in hot pursuit, creating a series of laps and pausing only to hear the other's 'first confession.'

She can also recall the day that granddad was on his way out the front door to go to the bank (The Bank of Ireland, Market Square, Navan), when granny admonished him for wearing his old dungarees. My mother never forgot by way of defence his response, 'Maggie, those who know me know I have better, and those who don't know me, don't give a damn!'

My mother's love for horticulture and first introduction to into the world of commerce began when she was twelve years old, selling organic vegetables from the family garden.

She gained an interest in gardening at a young age, from watching granddad sowing spring vegetable seed and planting early potatoes. When she was older, she cycled from her home accompanied by her sister Carmel to buy her first packet of seeds from McNamara's seed store in Drogheda.

York cabbage, lettuce, scallions (White Lisbon), cucumber, tomatoes and peas (when in season) were soon supplied to the two hotels in Navan, Crinnion's, Market Square and The Russell Arms Hotel, Bridge St Kappock's and O'Hagans, Trimgate St and Sheridan's Watergate St were shops that would order and collect the fresh vegetables daily by carrier bike and make up to two or three collections on a Saturday. In addition to this, Lightfoot the auctioneer's, Smithfield Market, Dublin ordered 200 heads of lettuce every Tuesday and Friday, which were collected at her door by the CIE bus en route to Dublin.

Granddad made a large timber box with netting wire acting as a lid to help transport the produce; he had also built a greenhouse to help generate her thriving business.

The Junior Red Cross held a dual purpose for my mother and her sister Carmel, not only did they learn' first aid' on a Wednesday night, they also became absentee's from its Friday night meetings, dancing along to the cheile and old time waltzes in the O'Mahony's instead. When it came to time to 'leave the meeting' the worn out dancers would then sprint home from Brew's Hill, Navan to their front door in Athlumney in less than seven minutes.

Although it became fashionable for women to wear trousers in Europe and certainly in movie-making Hollywood in the early forties, very few women in Navan ventured to wear them, my mother at least being the exception at least while gardening. One day while in the garden wearing her father's 'borrowed' black wool trousers stylishly tied with twine, a priest friend of the family happened by. Frantic to escape from him and avoid being seen wearing 'britches' and her father's britches at that, she hides herself (of all places) behind the greenhouse door. Granddad finally intervened with laughter, 'Come on out from behind the 'curtains' of that greenhouse,' he chuckled, 'and give us a twirl.'

My granddad died of a sudden illness on 14 September1954 aged seventy.

One of the most interesting and unusual incidents relating to my grandfather

Even the last resting place of poet FR Higgins in Laracor churchyard has to accommodate a proliferation of cow parsley.

Everything from ice cream to football boots were on offer when Drumree Stores were in business.

The village of Dunshaughlin in the early 1900s.

A traffic-free Dunshaughlin in the 1950s.

happened some twenty years after his death. In the early 1970s while removing the wainscoting in the hall of the old house, one of the panels of wood was noted to have some writing in pencil on it. On closer inspection it read:

Christopher O'Brien
Died 14th September, 1954
R.I.P.

Nothing out of the ordinary about that perhaps, except for the fact that it was written unmistakably in granddad's own hand writing as later confirmed by his three daughters and that moreover the wainscoting had not been disturbed since Granddad himself had first panelled it in the 1930s.

Naturally while about any carpentry work my grandfather always carried a flat carpenter's pencil behind his ear. Could he have predicted the date, month and year of his own death?

Louise Scott

Michael Cassidy's Slane

Michael Cassidy, who sadly is no longer with us, was surely one of the greatest storytellers ever to come from the Slane area. Having travelled the world his interests were varied and include, in his own words, such subjects as history, horse riding, art, painting and above all a deep interest in his fellow human beings. In the mid-1990s I had the privilege of publishing one of his short stories.

His untimely death deprived the world of a wealth of stories about life in rural Meath.

In listing his cultural interests, Michael Cassidy was at pains to highlight one particular area of interest, namely 'People and their Environment.'

Very few people that I met during my lifetime would have made such a lasting impression on me as Michael Cassidy. Born and reared in Slane, Michael received his early education in Slane National School. The early part of his working life was spent in Dublin. From Dublin he moved to London and after that to France where he studied restaurant operation and of course the language. He continued his studies in Switzerland and indeed began to study business management.

Returning to Ireland in 1959 he worked in Dublin, Cork and Killarney in Hotel Management before eventually retiring to his native Slane.

Michael always had a keen interest in travel and during his travelling years he made it to a number of cities throughout the world, including San Francisco, San Diego, Palm Beach, Capistrano, New York and Boston. He had many hobbies and pastimes and these ranged from the cultural and historic to sports.

One of the great delights of his later years was writing and nothing pleased him better than to see his work in print. I was privileged to be in a position to publish some of his work in an anthology. He was at his best however, when writing about his native Slane. So let us listen to the voice of Michael Cassidy as he recalls some of the characters that he knew.

Here he tells us about some of the characters that he knew during his days in Slane local characters. The first of these is a character called Christy Clinton.

Christy Clinton was a travelling workman who got employment from farmers in the Creewood and Davidstown area. He was a smallish bearded man who wore a cap and was about fifty years old. He took very long strides and always used a stick for walking, a most colourful character who worked the day in Main Street, Slane, when he came into the village. Kathleen and Andy Blake gave him work cleaning out sheds, stables and washing beer bottles for perhaps two or three days. He never asked for payment but he was well fed and Blakes gave him some ale and stout to drink in their pub without charge. His banter was rich, innocent and entertaining. He worked only in three or four houses, sawing sticks for firewood and sweeping around the yard. He also did some brushing, a little garden work and general outside cleaning for a few shillings and a meal.

Christy Clinton died in the late fifties and the farmers gave him a decent burial. A remarkable rural personality had passed on.

Jack Kinsella

In the early 1930s Jack Kinsella lived up the Dublin Road a few miles from Slane. He could be heard long before you saw him arrive with his strong staccato voice, dressed like an army officer with riding breeches, polished brown leggings and boots to match, a smart tweed country jacket he was a model of smartness for his job in hand. He came to Pat Meade the butcher to train broken down racehorses for carting and light farm work. Pat Meade delivered baskets of meat to the big houses around Slane, otherwise the broken down pure-breds worked on Pat Meade's farm in Cashel.

Jack Kinsella's brief was to train the horses for the cart, horses that could forget the cheering crowds of the grand stands, the parade rings and the racecourses and knuckle under a cartload of meat and Jack Kinsella was the man for the task. You could not see a better performance at Duffy's circus, the long rope traces behind the horse firmly in Jack's hands and he shouting instructions to the elegant colt in front.

The breaking and training took place in the yard, the paddock and finally on the road.

If the horse bolted in the cart Jack would leap on the horses back and in a flash regain control of the animal. It was a joy to see Jack Kinsella at work. If you made eye contact with him he would complain about the colt's particular fault, 'but I'll put manners on him and teach him who the boss is,' and that he did much to Pat Meade's satisfaction.

Ned Corrigan

Ned Corrigan was a colourful character to look at, dressed in a frock coat with a waistcoat decorated with a watch chain from the right pocket to the left pocket, where the watch lodged. Leggings and boots, black polished, shiny as new, Ned was seen mostly around the square. Edward (Ned) Corrigan died on 18 December1935.

If we cherish our past the present and future heritage will be cared for. It will be preserved for our future generations yet to come into this great cultural centre.

The Herd of Stanley Hill

He was gentle, kind and generous to all that knew him and that included young, medium and old folks. Those who knew Paddy O'Brien were privileged to be a friend of his. Paddy was a herd on the Stanley Hill farm owned by Sam (Samuel) in McKeever of Fennor. It was a big farm of more than 200 acres of great grazing land.

Mr McKeever changed the stock grazing the farm every few months from the Fennor farm that may have been for fattening and finishing livestock before export. The quality and breeds of cattle were the highest standards, Sam McKeever would not settle for anything less than the best.

Paddy O'Brien walked the farm morning and evening, and the Wicklow collie 'Shep' went everywhere with Paddy. The herd of cattle was checked for head count and any illness in the animals. Most of the fields were named: The Chapel Field, Well Field, Football Field, The Pound, Woodfarm etc.. Occasionally there would be a maverick in the herd that broke out through a gap in the ditch and the bullock wandered off and got lost. It was Paddy's job to go out in search of the lost animal and not to give up the hunt 'till he found his lost soul.' It was a great joy and relief to find the lost bullock in the next farm or lost on the road miles away. Only a good herd would know some animal instincts to have some idea where the lost bullock would wander. Paddy O'Brien lived in the herd's house at the top of Chapel Lane, off Chapel Street between the two large houses beside the chapel. The house had several adjoining stables and a barn all surrounded by haggard, large pens for cattle sorting and outbuildings. Paddy's house was typical of the small farm house, the open grate, a stool on either side of the fireplace, the cross bar and chains with the hooks for the two pot ovens and the iron kettle. You could view the sky by looking up the chimney. There was a kitchen table, two or three chairs and a kitchen dresser. The bedroom may have been in the attic. The low window and shelf provided seating for two places. The small paraffin oil lamp had a wick trimmed and lighted. The glow from the fire and the soft light from the lamp embellished the chat and stories of Paddy's friends who called to his open house any night of the week. Paddy was a tall thin man with a moustache, a cloth cap and always the drover's stick.

His range of topics and conversation spread over a wide vista, just like his ranch from the top of Stanley Hill- as far as the eye could see and never a word of animosity about any living being. He was a delight to talk with and his wisdom knew no bounds. When the embers glowed low and faded in the grate it was time to depart without ever having to be told to. He enjoyed his friends calling to him and they enjoyed his lovely stories.

In the early 1930s the woman of the house rarely was seen outside the door of her home except for early mass on Sundays. Sitting around the fire listening to stories and yarns and events of the past from the older citizens was a normal past time in the light of a candle or paraffin oil lamp hanging on the wall. In the drawing room was a luxury pedestal oil lamp with a variegated shade and a double wick burner placed on the centre. The shops used Aladdin lamps with the mantle wick for a much stronger light.

The senior adults of the house went for a walk out the road as far as Harlinstown Cross, then turn back. The lone chestnut tree on the left near Harlinstown had a strange forbidding presence as you approached it in deathly silence, like there were strange spirits within the tree trunk looking out at these intruders walking past it. Autumn and winter times had the darkest imaginable sky at night. The castle gate entrance with the huge green doors shut showed a massive silhouette against the sky and trees on the sawmills side.

The castle hill lined with chestnut trees standing like sentinels on one side the very high wall of the castle garden on the other struck fear into the road walkers at night. There was a small green door at the top of the castle hill and there were no more trees from here to the hunters gate at the turn of the road near the concert entrance.

It is told that a big black hound often walked on the wall from the castle gate to the protestant church at certain times during the winter. This fearsome experience was told many times around the fire while the pig's pot and the spuds simmered away for hours.

Michael Cassidy

Moving to the Flatlands of County Meath

Moving to the flatlands of County Meath is something that many thousands of people have done in recent years. So big has been the influx of people into the county that the population of the county is much greater now than before the famine.

Frank Goodman came from Dublin and Tommy Farrell came from Galway. Both found a welcome in the Royal County.

I moved to the flatlands of the Royal County very close to the high kings of Tara who with their people greeted me with a warm smile.

I live at Raynestown, Dunshaughlin and it's been twenty-seven years since I moved here. Although the people of Dunshaughlin greeted me with a smile, I was also greeted with a cold shoulder by the weather. My six children were educated in the local Rathbeggan Primary school and moved on to the Community College in Dunshaughlin. Due to their schooling in Dunshaughlin some of them went on to third level and graduated.

Raynestown Lane is home to Rathregan Cemetery built in the year 1798 as highlighted on the entrance, no doubt home to some of the Irish rebels of that time. It is close to the village of Batterstown, a heritage town, frequented in times past by the man we now know as Saint Oliver Plunkett. Further down off the Trim road stands Culmullen Church, an architectural masterpiece frequented by those who appreciate its ancient heritage and design. Beside the entrance stands a monument erected by the people of Meath in remembrance of the rebels of 1798. Taking the road from Culmullen back to Dunshaughlin one passes the house where Michael Collins, another famous man of Irish history, stayed. Driving towards Raynestown on the Navan Road one can view the old Workhouse; a cut stone building built in the times of the famine. It was an effort by the people of Dunshaughlin to stave off starvation. Further on the Navan Road going towards Dublin can be viewed an old derelict house where it is reputed that Michael Collins also stayed.

Dunshaughlin in the year 1980 was a typical Irish village; it has since graduated to become a thriving busy town on the outskirts of Dublin. With its own business park with twenty premises employing upwards of two thousand people. An Ireland much changed for the better.

My neighbour Tommy Farrell, a Galway man who has since gone to his eternal reward, had come to reside at Raynestown in the mid-thirties where he lived with his wife Gretta and sons Anthony and Noel. His business was sheep farming. He was well known in County Meath for transporting breeding ewes from the west to the Trim market in the east, as seen in the photograph featured in the *Farmer's Journal* in the *Irish Independent* around the year 1968.

Walking past his farmyard one can still view the sheep pens used in those days - they could tell a tale of hard work and hard times. Tommy bought lambs for order and among his clients was at least one Dublin wholesaler. During the summer months he used to go to fairs in the west and buy breeding ewes. The sheep would be brought to

The original interior of what is now 'The Pepperpot' in Navan's Trimgate Street.

Lawlor's Bakery in Navan's Trimgate Street as it appeared in the 1960s.

Meath by lorry and then delivered to or collected by the local farmers. Orders could vary from ten to sixty depending on the size of the holding. He generally got paid at the rate of two shillings commission per head.

The old sheep pen, which he used to separate the sheep, still exists although in a very dilapidated state, and I'm sure it could tell many a tale of different incidents over the years. Things have changed a lot since then. I am indebted to his son Anthony for these insights into the life of a great sheep-man.

Frank Goodman

The Black and Tans

I was born and reared on a farm near the village of Dunderry, which is roughly halfway between Navan and Trim. My grandmother also had a farm, a small one also in Dunderry although she herself lived in Robinstown, which is about three miles distant from Dunderry. My grandfather's name was Ledwidge and at one stage during the Black and Tan campaign he owned a pub in Trim. This is now Leonard's Bar and Hardware at Athboy Gate. Back then it was known as Ledwidge's Pub and the Black and Tans used to drink there.

My grandfather was very wary of these customers, particularly one character called Jack, who used to follow people around the town abusing them and generally frightening them. When the town was burned by the Black and Tans my family had to take to the field or else they would be killed.

My father used to tell us about the lorry loads of Black and Tans that would pass by his farm in Dunderry shouting and terrorising anyone they would come across. They were, according to my father, looking for a man that was supposed to be in the IRA and they would search our farm several times looking for him. My father however, would send this man to another farm we had near the village of Rathoath so they never really caught up with him. This man was called Slevin and apparently he was a judge in the IRA. If they caught him they would certainly have killed him just like the two fellows that they caught walking along the Navan-Athboy road. They brought them out to Tullaghnstown bog and threw them in a bog hole and they were never seen again.

These were strange times according to my father and it wasn't unusual to meet men carrying arms at all hours of the day or night. They would just pass by with never as much as a word and we would go on our way and ask no questions.

I have my own memories of the farm in Dunderry and I remember that we would have all sorts of visitors from time to time. One character that I recall was called Jack and he would walk the roads around Dunderry singing and shouting at the top of his voice. My mother would bring him in and give him his dinner and he was off again. Then we had people coming out from Trim selling pots and pans. Decent honest people, they would always give you good value.

I remember how my mother would spend days getting ready for the threshing. The visit of the threshing mill was a great event on our farm. I remember too a travelling show coming to the village for two weeks in either October or November - the Jack Courtney Travelling Show from Wexford. We would be looking forward to it coming.

The old yews, Headfort, Kells, County Meath. Early 1900s.

The ruins at Newtown from the Echo Gate.

Fr Eoghan O' Growney

My grandfather had a cousin called Eugene O'Growney who lived near Athboy. At one stage he came to live with my grandfather in Dunderry. He studied in Navan for the priesthood, eventually becoming a priest. He learned the Irish language from a man called Rack who lived in a little thatched cottage near our farm. He eventually went on to hold the chair in Irish in Maynooth College. He went to America for the good of his health and died out there.

John Darcy

The Man from Maudlin Street

Tommy Grimes was elected to Kells Urban Council in 1973 and is still, according to his own words, 'privileged to represent the best people you could wish to meet.' Reproduced here is a detailed account of his early life growing up in Kells

I was born in Maudlin Street, in September 1946, the third eldest of ten, and my parents being Tommy and Mary Grimes (*née* Cummins). I had a great childhood with very good memories.

My late mother sent me to school when I was three and a half, as Christy and Jane were behind me, they maintained I was safer at school. Mother told the family afterwards that the Reverend Mother was sending home notes requesting my birth certificate for six months. The day I was four years old my mother sent in a birth certificate. The very first day I attended school, would you believe it, I was knocked down crossing the road by a bike.

Caffery's always had lorries outside their house, it was around 1951 and Sean Grace and myself got into one of the lorries and we were playing pulling levers and anything we could see when the lorry took off. Lucky for us it only went about ten yards when it struck an E.S.B. pole and came to a halt. Guard McKeown gave us a proper dressing down.

I remember Billy Dunne from Maudlin Bridge bringing in the milk every morning. We used to knock on the doors, get the cans from the women in the houses and collect the milk. Billy would always have sweets to hand out.

Another thing that I remember was when my uncle Paddy would come to town in the horse and cart after doing his business in Kells he would load us up in the cart and bring us to the railway gates and drops us off. We would have to walk home.

Every Saturday morning all the boys and girls would meet and go to Cherry Hill to collect firewood. Just imagine ten to twelve big branches being pulled in line - the dust was horrific with everyone running down the back road racing each other, bringing home the firewood.

In 1954 Meath won their second All Ireland, a neighbour in Maudlin, Michael Grace R.I.P., was the star man. We all marched from Grace's house in Maudlin to the Fair Green carrying sods of turf on forks and we all singing, 'Cheer up the Meath team, they're known everywhere, we beat down the Kerry team, we beat them lying there.' The family moved to St Colmcille's Villas in 1956. Just imagine, we were all looking at a bath and an indoor toilet for the first time. (Oh, what a thrill). Our next door neighbours were Gogarty's and Kinsella's.

Again memories were great, listening to Paddy Reilly taken on Michael O' Heither's commentary on the football games at Croke Park. We all used to gather at the four poles and listen to Paddy's brilliant voice, every player every position and every move spoke with such vigour; we would all cheer when Meath would score. I have often wondered if someone in authority heard Paddy, would he would have been on the radio.

My father looked after the waterworks for thirty-one years. Every morning Michael Black and he would arrive in for tea and I can remember them taking the mushrooms from their handkerchief that they had picked in Lloyd and putting them on the range when my mother would be making the tea.

The intake flowed from Clavins Bridge to the waterworks, then to the filter beds and was pumped up to the reservoir and pumped into the town. This intake would have to be cleaned every two years and casual staff would be taken on. The water would be blocked at the bridge to allow the workers to pull the weeds. A lot of fish would be found under the weeds and the men would throw all the fish up on to the bank. My brothers Pa and Christy would get the half day off school to gather the fish on the bank. At the end of the day all the fish would be shared and we would have a great feast. There were three days in the year when we were allowed off school:

16 October: the Big Fair Day

The Fat Stock Show

The Greyhound Coursing Meeting in Lloyd.

The Big Fair Day was part of Kells. I remember all the sheep in pens along the circular road, the cattle would be in Cannon Street and Castle Street and the horses would be in Farrell Street. We would all gather in Farrell Street to listen to 'Cheap John'.

The Fat Stock Show would take place in the Gaelic grounds. I remember the cattle being from the Gaelic grounds to the trains. There would be three or four trains all loaded up and transported away.

Coursing was held in the month of January in Loyd. Prior to the actual coursing meeting, we would all meet on Sunday morning to catch the hares. Some of the people that I remember being over the coursing at that time were Jimmy Murray, Tommy Morris, Jim Sweeney, Bob Tormey, Jimmy Reilly and Jack Olohan.

Kells was a great place to grow up in the fifties. I remember joining the boxing club, winning the Meath Championships and reaching the Leinster finals in Athlone. My late father would not allow me to box as I had a dental appointment the next day and I was very disappointed.

Everyone shared what we had, which was not a lot. My mates at the time, David Geraghty, Sean Grace, Thomas McManus, Michael Reilly, Patsy Byrne, Dessie McGovern, Dermot Grimes R.I.P. and many more would meet at the handball club and play there for hours. In 1957 Paddy Duff, Michael Black and Willie Black and others founded The Kells Handball Club. I remember all the men gathering at the club and cleaning the whole area. At that time four families lived where the alley is now, Ned Sheridan, Jimmy Reilly, Star Man Bell and Paddy Reilly. Church Lane was known as the street of champions- Tormey's, Grime's, Bells, Sheridan's, and McGovern's, Molly's, McConnell's and the O'Reilly's - all of these won All Ireland's, some even going abroad to represent Ireland. The club is still producing young players such as Gary McConnell and Brian Carroll (long may it continue.)

Running home from school at twelve forty-five for dinner, listening to the Kennedy's of Castle Ross on Fridays, everyone had concannon for dinner, and afterwards rice or sago with a large chunk of jam in the middle. But the real treat was on a Saturday with two pound of Hopkin's sausages. Jimmy Sheridan. R.I. P. was the local butcher, a lovely man who always looked after the ordinary people. Mother would be cooking sausages, you had big and small ones and I would be first to grab the big one and all hell would break loose.

Other things we would get up to were setting night lines for fish and snouting for eels and hunting rabbits was a great pastime. I will always remember Bosco Rourke tickling trout at the Pidgeon Rock in Maudlin.

The formation of Kells Celtic A.F.C. brings back memories, local lads playing soccer in Monaghans, Moynalty Road, and Maudlin Street and later on at the Red Hills. I could never understand grown men looking over the hedge from the road, taking names and expelling boys from the G.A.A.

Mondays were the wash days with pots of washing from early morning. I remember mother waiting for an elderly man, Thady Clarke, to find out the weather forecast. Thady would look up at the sky and advise her either to hang out the washing or wait. Until her final days she maintained he was always correct. Unfortunately Mr Clarke lost his life in a house fire.

Joe Cooney and Eddie Guerin went to serve a wedding on a Friday in Lent. They got the half-day off from school but when they returned Brother Kiely called the two boys up to the front of the class and asked them who had got married and how much they got for serving at the wedding. After answering all the questions there was blue murder because no one got married in Lent that time.

On wintry night sitting around the fire and mother reading 'Kitty the Hare' from Our Boys, just imagine being told ghost stories at seven or eight years of age and having to go to bed. The truth is that mother had to sleep with us until we fell asleep. (A wonderful person and a great mother).

I started work in the bakery August in 1960, my bosses were John Maxwell, Peter Smyth and Charles Stuart Parnell Geraghty, three lovely people. John will always have a special place with me as he always stood up for me and never allowed anyone to bully me. I remember Bob Tormey coming into the bakery and collecting union dues.

I met my wife Ann (née Yore) in 1963 and we were married in 1968. We had four children, Helen, Gillian, Alan and Laura. We are now the proud grandparents of Cellaigh, Evan, Sophie, Jack, Caithlain and Laragh.

Tommy Grimes

The Tom Darby Story

The Tom Darby story is all about music - accordion music, pipe music and the music of the drum and of course the bagpipes. Meath always had enough musicians to ensure that a band could be formed at any time in any one of a dozen different locations around the county. Tom Darby originally came from Slane where he was born and remained until he was four and a half years of age. Here Tom tells the story himself.

Yes I was born in Slane where I remained until I was four and a half years of age when we moved to Fennor. I lived in Fennor until 1962 when I got married to Theresa and moved here to Dean Hill to where I have been living happily ever since. We had five children in all, two sons and three daughters. I worked for the Slane Manufacturing company for seventeen years.

I worked with Marty Johnson in the pub for seven years and actually played with the famous Johnson sisters, well actually two sisters and the brother. Marty himself went on to be a TD in the Dáil. Then I had been interested in music since I was no more than six years of age playing the drums would have been my first attempt. Both my mother and father were accomplished musicians especially on the accordion. They preferred the button key accordion.

As long as I can remember my family had always been involved in the Slane Carnival. I suppose all this was laying the foundations for my lifelong love of music.

Then in 1954 I founded the famous Darby brother's band with my brothers Packie and Martin. Packie of course is no longer with us, God be good to him, while Martin went on to be a regular on the LM/FM Saturday morning programme *The Green Scene.*

I also play the tin whistle and the drums and even the bagpipe. We actually started a pipe band in Beauparc. St Martin's Pipe band it was called after our generous benefactor Mr Riddle Martin. I was a drummer in that band.

We would run afternoon dances on Sunday afternoons in Rathkenny Hall and we would use any money that we would make to fund St. Martin's Pipe band. When St Martin's pipe band did eventually fold up a lot of the pipers moved to the Kentstown band.

I suppose you played with a lot of famous people over the years, I suggested.

Oh, indeed I did. I remember particularly playing with Dermot O'Brien and then there was Paddy Cole and Tom Duff. Tom's daughter, the well-known singer Mary Duff, is a wonderful singer and the very first time that I heard her sing I was sure that she would go to the top. I actually told her as much. Another very famous musician that I played for was Jack Barret from Kells. He was actually a well-known bandleader and I played with him in England.

I also played with the Joe Tolan Céile band and we travelled far and wide even as far as Galway and Salthill.

One incident that I recall was the time that the Somerville Pipers left myself and Marty Johnson in charge of the pipes and drums. We of course got hold of them and played up and down the street in Slane – Marty on the bagpipes and me on the drum. All the people in the village came out to see us and it was great fun and everyone enjoyed it.

I suppose I am as busy as I ever was now, what with playing for different groups, senior citizen's and active retirement groups and then in nursing homes. Then there is the Donore Interpretative Centre and Slane and even this very morning I was playing at an active retirement Valentine party over in Yellow Furze Parish Hall.

From September every year things really get busy with Christmas parties and then doing Santa in the pubs. I played in the Lantern public house in Navan twenty-seven years and I still do, usually accompanied by my old friend Tom Duff. Then I also have the odd session with banjo player Seán Maguire in the Haggard in Trim. The Trim Senior Citizens in the hotel is another place where I am likely to play occasionally.

I worked for the Meath Sheltered Workshop for thirteen years driving the

Meath County Council Dance in the CYMS Hall, Navan in the early 1960s.

The old and the new – the ruins of the old cathedral in the church grounds, Trim.

handicapped patients here and there and every day I would never fail to give them a few bars on the accordion.

Interview with Tom Darby at his home in Dean Hill, February 2006.

Three Characters

The three voices featured in the following anecdotes belong to characters that have long since gone to their eternal reward. They belong to Jim Mahon, a bookies clerk from Navan, Tommy (Gus) McCormack who in the 1940s worked in Spicer's Bakery and Porky Williams, who was a popular bread van driver for Spicer's.

For most of the twentieth century there were just two bookies serving the town of Trim and the surrounding area; located on either side of the main street, Harte on the same side as J & E Smyth's and Finnegan's on the same side as Christum Leonard's Hardware.

I backed my horses with Finnegan's. Jim Mahon, a Navan man, ran this office and he was a familiar sight on the Navan Road where he did the double journey every day summer and winter. He carried all the dockets and betting slips and of course the cash in a small suitcase strapped to the saddle of his Rudge bicycle.

Meath Diocesan pilgrimage to Lourdes, 9 to 14 May 1969.

Even when your horses lost Jim would have a word of consolation.
'You were in hard luck with that one, Tom,' *or* 'Well at least you had him each way,' *or,*
'I see your horse is running tomorrow and he might be worth a bob or two.'

One of my earliest recollections of being involved with the horses is of one particular Saturday when I was working in Spicer's yard. Spicer's was a great place for the horses then and nearly every day someone would have a tip for a horse. I was in conversation with Tommy (Gus) McCormack when the telegram boy wheeled in the gate and handed me a telegram. Filled with anticipation I proceeded to open it and read the message. It read 'Rashas in the 2pm at Kempton Park'.

'It's a tip,' *Gus informed me.* 'Let's look at the paper. Never ignore a tip, we could be in the money here Tom, let's go and get the paper.'

Having confirmed that there was actually a horse called Rashas running in the two p.m. at Kempton Park I lost no time in informing anyone who would care to listen to me. The result was that by the time the race was off most of the townsfolk had a few bob on the horse. I put ten bob on it and history will show that Rashas finished last at 33/1.

Yes, I was embarrassed and not a little hurt that anyone would send away for a tip in my name and the fact that I was almost certain that the culprit was a certain portly bread van driver didn't make it any easier. For weeks after he would greet me with the words 'Any good tips lately' *or* 'what do you fancy today Tom?'.

At least I was wiser and when some weeks later I received another telegram, this time with a tip for a horse called Blackpool Tower in the three p.m. at Haydock, I tore up the telegram and put it in the bin. I never mentioned it to a soul, not even my friend Gus McCormack. Blackpool Tower romped home an easy winner at 100/8. For weeks after that I received demands from the tipster in Sutton Coldfield in England. However I threw them all in the bin and eventually they ceased.

four

Occupations

A Picturesque Village

It is generally accepted that the village of Summerhill in south Meath is one of the most beautiful villages to be found anywhere in Ireland. Perfectly laid out with its village green in the centre the structure of the village has changed little over the years. This is also the opinion expressed by former village postmistress Phyllis Gogarty when I spoke with her in the old post office building in January 2006. Miss Gogarty is a direct descendant of Bernardo O'Higgins who is widely revered in Chile and indeed throughout South America.

As a young girl I would often hear my parents talking about the family connection with Ambrose and Bernardo O'Higgins.

The Langford family were the important people in the village in the old days and it was the Langfords that actually laid out the village and a right good job they made of it too. Miss Gogarty was loud in her praise for these old time planners.

The huge two-storey building that used to house the post office was originally occupied by a Presbyterian minister called Craig. Another family came after Craig before we took it over. It was a Presbyterian meeting house then but as far as I can recall from hearing people talk there was some kind of difference between the Presbyterians and the Church of Ireland. The building is actually two buildings in one. There was the post office and the private building. My family is from the area but I am a native of the village and except when I was away at boarding school I have been here all my life.

Besides having a post office we had a drapery attached and later on we sold groceries and sweets.

You were the post mistress here, I said.

Indeed I was since around the 1960s. It was my mother that kept the post office before that but she seldom stood in it as she had an assistant and indeed sometimes two when the post office would be extra busy.

There was no such thing as children's allowances then and people were very poor but they were happy and apparently they didn't feel deprived despite the lack of money.

Children then didn't hold as much stock on money as they do today and I remember my father used to give me a pound note for my birthday and then he would insist that I put in it my post office saving account. Actually I didn't always put it in the post office savings bank because I remember once getting a scissors and cutting out the figure of Lady Laverty. Of course this would render the note useless but at least I would have the satisfaction of having cut the figure out perfectly.

I remember just how busy we were back in the old days especially when the fair was on. There would be four main fairs in the village every year and people used to time their business to coincide with the fair.

There were no such things as telephone kiosks in them days and very few people had a phone so that all calls would have to be made from our post office. We had a huge cabinet much like an indoor kiosk and the farmers and their wives would be using the phone constantly.

Summerhill had a population of less than 150 back then and I remember one particular character called Jack Mannion. Jack, God be good to him, was decent man and a cattle drover. He drove herds of cattle all over the county then and of course to the station in Enfield. During all the time he was driving cattle he never lost a beast. He was known far and wide and was on first name terms with some of the big band leaders of the day including Johnny Butler and Pat Jackson.

You must have seen many changes in the village during your life here, I suggested.

Well it's hard to recognise it now from what it was. Most of the buildings have changed and we have a new post office.

Interview with former postmistress of Summerhill, January 2006.

Bibi's Story

In my younger days I worked in Owen's Dairy in Slane. It was situated about a mile from Slane at a place called Harding's Cross and not far from the river. There were no cows attached to this dairy and the farmers around the area brought in the milk and it was then poured into big stainless steel containers. I suppose there would have been about forty people working there in my time and we would work a seventy hour week for a pound an hour. We would begin work at nine a.m. and we wouldn't finish until eight p.m.

My job was to regulate the amount of milk that went into each bottle. These were the pint bottles that we all remember. Someone else would have the job of putting the caps on the bottles - white caps for buttermilk and red caps for ordinary milk. I remember some of those that worked there, particularly Ann Kennedy who did the accounts and made up the wages. Another person that I vividly recall is Henry Cassidy. He would come in to fix the machines when they would break down.

Bibi White.

Days off School

What Paddy Duffy doesn't know about life in rural Meath in the 1950s and 60s is hardly worth knowing. It was actually during an interview with him in May 2006 that I learned quite a bit about harvesting myself. When it comes to describing a day at the threshing mill or a day planting or picking potatoes the Robinstown farmer is in his element. In the following piece Paddy tells of how in his young days he would be kept at home from school to help with the varied and seasonal jobs around the farm.

When I was a young boy going to primary school and most of the class would have come from a farming background, at certain times of the year we could get days off from school for the planting and harvesting of potatoes. This would be in early April and in September.

At the planting stage the ground would be tilled and the drills risen. We would then proceed to load the farmyard manure, or dung as it was more popularly called, where it would be taken out to the field and deposited in heaps along the drills. That would take most of the first day or most of the second day. Our hands would be well blistered by the time we had the dung out. The next day it would be up at dawn and out to spread the dung evenly in every drill. This would complete the second day. Then on the third day we would have aching bones but despite this the planting would begin. The horse and cart would be loaded up with bags of seed potatoes and deposited in three or four locations along the field. Every available able-bodied member of the family or any neighbour that could be persuaded to help out would then begin the task of dropping the potatoes foot lengths apart. As youngsters we would never take the work too seriously and we would have some fun throwing the seed potatoes at each other.

At dinnertime we would be called to the house for the main meal which would usually consist of bacon and cabbage while the man with the horse and plough would be closing in the drills that had been planted.

With dinner over it would be back to the field with stiff backs from all the stooping and we would proceed to finish the planting. If we weren't finished by around four in the afternoon, my mother would bring out tea and bread and jam, complicated by the youngsters throwing clods at each other. This would continue until somebody would come and reprimand us. Anyway, with the planting finished we would have to clean up. The clean up however, would be of a temporary nature until we could have proper wash later.

Have you any memories of days spent on the bog, I asked Paddy.

Yes indeed, turf cutting was another activity that we had to help out with during these days off although we didn't actually have a turf bank we would be expected to help out with the neighbours either at catching and stacking on the bog barrows. Then some of the heavier built grown ups would come and wheel it away and scatter it out on the spread bank to dry. This operation would take about one week and it was then back to our lessons.

It would be August or September before we could expect to get another day off, although we would have to spend most of our spare time thinning turnips and mangolds and weeding the potatoes. Come September however, our next job would be harvesting the corn and this might last but a day or two. We could be sure of getting a day off for this if it happened during the school term. It would be a similar story with the threshing although we wouldn't have any part in the actual drawing in of the corn and we wouldn't be kept away from school for the drawing of the corn.

There would be plenty of jobs for us youngsters at the mill: jobs such as cutting the twine off the sheaves, handing the open sheaf to the man feeding the mill. This exercise required it to be done correctly as sometimes the man pitching up the sheaves would hand them the wrong way and this would be our job to turn it the right way, which tended to slow up the work.

Then we used to take turns at keeping the chaff away for the mill, although being youngsters we would have great fun throwing chaff at each other. In the old days this chaff would be used to make mattresses while any that was left over would be burned.

St Oliver's new church, Oldcastle, as it appeared in 1905.

The interior of the Catholic church, Oldcastle in 1935.

St Joseph's Convent of Mercy, Navan, away from the clamour and the noise. A scene from the early part of the twentieth century.

The straw from the milling operation would be stacked into a huge stack and this was a job that required as many as ten men. It would take another three men to catch the corn in barrel sacks and carry it to the store. Some of those sacks could weigh as much as twenty stone and still the men would be expected to carry them sometimes up a ladder to the loft.

Of course we would get our reward in the shape of plenty of Taylor Keith lemonade and Marietta biscuits which we would tuck into with gusto.

Our final couple of days off for the year would be for the harvesting of the potatoes. Seeing that there would be ten times more potatoes to be picked than there had to be planted, this obviously was much harder work. Still we always had time for the mandatory pranks such as putting stones in someone else's bag or throwing clods. This was part of the fun of it all.

Although we weren't involved in the storing or pitting of the potato harvest we were well aware that it was an essential part of the whole operation. This operation meant drawing the potatoes into the haggard where they would be kept until there was an opportunity to pit them properly. We didn't see any of this because by the time this was done we would be immersed in our lessons once again and we couldn't expect to have another day off until the 8 December when we might get to Dublin for a day's shopping.

Interview with Paddy Duffy in May 2006

End of Tradition

A postal tradition stretching back to the nineteenth century in Rathfeigh came to an end recently when the local post office closed its doors for the last time. Postmistress Kay Halligan who ran the post office since 1977 stamped her last letter on Friday as she retired amidst tributes and good wishes from the local community.

Her departure from behind the counter of the post office means that Rathfeigh will no longer have a post office as An Post continues to streamline its services and cut down on rural post offices.

The closure of Rathfeigh Post Office means that there are now only twelve post offices left in the Navan area, which stretches from Ballivor and Clonmellon over to Lobinstown and Slane and up to Tara. Five years ago there were twenty-one.

The decline in the number of post offices means that the Navan and Kells branches of the Irish Postmasters Union are to amalgamate and will be holding their first general meeting as a joint body soon.

The first postmaster recorded in Rathfeigh was Nicholas Cromwell, in 1887 who ran a post office quite close to the present premises. In 1905 Rose Ann McLoughlin, who was a teacher in the local national school, ran the post office where her sister, Lena was based. The post office operated from the teacher's residence and Rose Ann later married James Madden.

The Grotto, St Joseph's of Mercy, Navan. Silent now, nearly a century since this picture was taken.

Michael 'The Sheriff' Sheils.

John Smyth and his son John Jr in the reconstructed version of the Forge. Notice the leather apron in the centre of the picture which was worn by Gussie.

The next person in charge of the mailing system was Teresa Dunne, mother-in-law of Kay Halligan, who ran it from the 1920s until her marriage to Eugene Halligan in 1936.

Up until then the post office was operating from the teacher's residence but when Minnie Gray became postmistress in 1936 it moved to Edoxtown. However, it wasn't long before it was back in Rathfeigh in 1942 when Marty Malone became postmistress. She ran it until 1973 when her sister, Elizabeth Swan took over in a temporary position. Kay Halligan took over in 1977.

There's been a tremendous change since then, Kay said last week. The currency changeover to the euro, as well as the earlier splitting of the Department of Posts and Telegraphs, were amongst the major changes she cited.

Other changes included the Department of Posts and Telegrams splitting up into the An Post and Eircom companies and the centralisation of sorting of mail from Tara to Navan and more recently to Dublin. Long-term postmen and women in Rathfeigh included Mattie Lynch and Joan Gallagher.

Among those to see Kay Halligan off were local schoolchildren who all brought letters to be stamped on Rathfeigh Post Office's last day, accompanied by teachers Phil McAuley, Seamus Tansley and Mary Luddy. Neighbours and locals also dropped in to wish Kay well, as did the current area postman Martin County.

John Donohoe

Missing the Buzz

Talking to Kay Halligan shortly after the closing of the post office I got the distinct feeling that she missed the excitement of running a rural post office with all the daily contacts and banter that goes with it.

I suppose seeing the post office as it is now closed down I am bound to feel a little sad. I was under no pressure to go and I appreciate the extra bit of time to myself. Deep down however I know that I have done the right thing.

True there is a bit of a vacuum in my life now but I will get used to it in time.

I feel sorry for the pensioners. They came here regularly to collect their pensions and in fact it was more of a social occasion for them as they met and had the chat and exchanged words about the weather. Some of them actually shed a tear at the closing of the post office. The idea of having their pensions paid directly into the bank wouldn't appeal to them and still less having to draw it from an ATM machine. They wouldn't like the new technology and to tell you the truth I wouldn't be gone on it myself. They will have to go elsewhere now to collect their pensions, Tara probably would be the nearest.

Interview with Kay Halligan, January 2006.

Fifty years of Medicine in County Meath

Now retired Ann McEntee's fascinating account of her medical experiences in County Meath and particularly in the village of Summerhill where she ran the local dispensary, will be of great interest to readers.

Ann, of course, is not new to the world of writing, having previously had a short story published. However, it is in her account of life as a GP in a small rural village County Meath that she excels.

We read about the day-to-day running of a facility that to most people would have very little knowledge of. It is all so new and strange and so far removed from today's world of mobile phones and instant communications.

It is the story of a struggle against the odds. It is the story of long hours and of a time when a reliable car was a luxury. It is just a little bit more that an ordinary account of life in County Meath in the past.

I grew up in Gorey, County Wexford. I qualified in medicine, in RCSI, Dublin in 1950 before marrying and moving to County Meath in 1952. Before I portray how it was to practice medicine in County Meath, it is useful to give an overview of how medical services in County Meath functioned at that time. So I will start with my life as a general practitioner, wife and mother in Trim.

My husband, Dr Larry, had worked with Dr Connie O'Reilly for six years living in *Mornington House*, Trim. At that time Dr Connie's brother, the Registrar, lived at *The Laurels*, Trim. Due to prolonged illness it was decided that if the Registrar left hospital he should live with Dr Connie and we could have this house and most of the furnishings. *The Laurels* came with the housekeeper 'Old Mary', Paddy Mooney who came daily to pump the water and his wife Molly who was available when needed. This was the domestic scene when I came to Trim.

My husband looked after the County Home (now St Joseph's Hospital), the Maternity Hospital and some of Dr Connie's private practice. Cars were scarce at that time and the telephone unreliable. The Maternity Hospital serviced the whole of County Meath for normal deliveries. A year or two later we got permission from the county council to 'hold' the ambulance, that is the ambulance would wait while the patient was seen and then take them on to Dublin if necessary. Previously all patients had to be admitted and the ambulance would have to return if a transfer was required. It was a red-letter day when Holles Street Hospital started their flying squad – direct ambulance complete with consultant – and could come to Meath.

The arrangements with Navan Hospital were equally difficult. There was a consultant who looked after everything. There was no county clinic, no clinics of any kind, no orthopaedics, no registrars, no office in the hospital – just a girl in the hall who answered the phone. All patients went straight to the ward or stayed at home until a bed was available. We were lucky in Trim that we inherited an excellent arrangement from Dr Connie who had a link with Mr Pringle in Baggot Street Hospital. The Pringle family came from Kilmessan originally. We sent Mr Pringle all out surgical referrals.

Most of my work in those days was to give the anaesthetics for my husband in the Maternity Hospital for forceps deliveries, open ether. I was also available for any emergency that he could not reach and I stood in for him on Sundays and other odd

Above left: With the statue of St Patrick gone from the summit of the Hill of Tara, the Lia Fail now stands alone.

Above right: Donaghmore Round Tower near Navan, evidence of our monastic past.

days. At least twice a week there were night calls to the maternity that implicated me. For my first few years Dr Connie was available on a Sunday provided I got him in time as he went visiting at five p.m. Some things I will never forget - stitching hurlers on a Sunday afternoon and then cycling up to the Maternity Hospital about four p.m. to check on the patients.

So much for the work side, on the social side, the tennis club in the grounds of the castle provided much entertainment with two excellent courts. Among our circle of friends, tennis in the summer was the focus for Sunday afternoon parties. The tennis started about three p.m. with a break for afternoon tea at five p.m. and about eight p.m. dinner followed by poker. I had a good excuse to absent myself-small babies–and I usually left about ten thirty p.m.. I know how to play poker but had the sense to pretend ignorance.

Summerhill

In March 1968 I was appointed to Summerhill dispensary. For some years previously it had been cared for by different locums. Summerhill was a large dispensary area with an almost non-existent phone service. From March to September 1968 I stayed in *Shandon House* odd nights and the younger members of the family enjoyed coming with me and 'camping'. The family moved to Summerhill in September but we retained the Trim practice where my husband worked. At that time 'Dispensary Days' in Summerhill were on Monday and Thursday. On Wednesday we had a small surgery in Rathmoylan, held in a cottage.

With the help of Dr Eilish Ridge, we decided to incorporate Summerhill and Trim as one practice. And so the Summerhill surgery was held in the morning and Trim in the afternoon. This arrangement was greatly assisted by the radiophone in my car whereby I was able to relay a lot of the messages to the secretary in Trim. Having come from a busy but well-organised practice, Summerhill presented some teething problems. There was no pretence of an office or charts or reports. My earliest recollection is of huge numbers of men who leaned against the surgery door and fell in when it was opened. Dispensing was done on the premises. This presented great difficulty for me initially as it meant having to order stock six weeks before it was required. The nearest chemist was in Trim but in Summerhill we were responsible for all medications needed by dispensary patients. It took years to get the patients trained to send in calls early. My predecessor in Summerhill, an elderly man, played golf in the morning and was happy to see patients or do house calls in the evenings.

Once we took up residence in Summerhill the assistant lived in Trim and life was easier. I had a great housekeeper, Nell Fitzpatrick, who knew the area and the people. In time we had a part-time secretary, Bridie Comey, and got a phone installed in the office. Summerhill continued as part of the Trim practice and this proved a good working arrangement. Bridie later became full-time, proving invaluable and is still working in the practice today.

The Working Week

So what was a week like in Summerhill? Surgery started at nine a.m. and we locked the door hopefully at noon. After lunch there were house calls, up to eight or nine p.m. in those days. The radiophone in my car was invaluable in this regard. Frequently I got to a house before the messenger had returned from making the phone call. I remember one day getting to a house by accident as I started my list of calls at the wrong end and decided to keep going. In the house a child had been badly scalded minutes before I arrived. I can still see the picture of disorder and feel the desperation of the mother and granny. With the radiophone I was able to summons an ambulance quickly and get permission from Navan to send the child straight to Dublin. Thankfully the outcome was good.

In the evening I might see two or three more patients. I did not encourage them as my energy was by that time on the wane. Tuesday was my half day, one p.m. to midnight. For weekends off I alternated with our assistant in Trim. Every Saturday there was a morning surgery in Summerhill, and an afternoon one in Trim. On Sundays we saw patients at noon - maybe five or six. This had the advantage of keeping the practice quiet for a few hours unless there was a football match.

The Book of Kells – further evidence of our monastic past.

Living in Summerhill

Summerhill is a small village. In 1968 it had one pub and one grocery shop that included a butcher and had a petrol pump. Since then things have moved on. Now there is an excellent large supermarket, a café, a chemist, and a butcher's shop, a pub serving lunches and a community centre, which has a bar licence for functions.

One of the nice things about Summerhill was the fact that almost everybody belonged to the practice, so in a way we were a 'family' and the practice was at the heart of it. I was fortunate that we had a Parish Priest with whom I had worked some years previously. He was very clever, kind and witty and our work frequently overlapped. In the '70s a chemist came to the village, a great asset from my point of view. My district nurse was a gem and completed this wonderful team who gave 'care' to the community. I remember one year when we had a really bad snow. The local sergeant insisted on accompanying me on a call. He brought along another man with some shovels. The first road we tried was blocked by a solid wall of snow five feet high.

The alternative route was passable with the help of our shovels. The health of my car was also very important to the practice and I was blessed with a first class mechanic and never got stuck.

In those days getting a patient admitted to hospital frequently meant organising somebody to mind the children. My nurse helped with this. I can remember a distraught old lady who would not go to hospital unless her dog was taken care of. The dog remained with me until the ambulance had come and gone. I recall an elderly man who had never stood in hospital who had a coronary and needed to be admitted. I ordered the ambulance and when I knew it was time for it to arrive, I told him that he needed an X-ray and did not hold it against me later when he found himself on a ward.

One had to be very careful about accepting gifts from patients. However, gifts of brown bread, potatoes, eggs, flowers and plants were always acceptable. When my husband died suddenly in 1973 the house was coming down with gifts of food and drink and there was a constant flow of patients who prepared meals, washed up and looked after the children. They literally took over the running of the house for days. The same applied to the practice. Previous locums got in touch and offered their services. It was very rewarding and consoling.

How does all this compare with medicine today? To illustrate what I feel, I'll tell a little story. Years ago I was talking to a local auctioneer who said 'When I'm unsure of a client I make an excuse to call to their house without an appointment. In a very short time I get the feel of the situation'. Personally the same applies to myself as I find it much easier to judge a patient and their progress with a house call. If I'm puzzled by the patient's story and I feel that there is something going on at home, a house call is useful and revealing.

Medicine has progressed greatly over the fifty years since I first came to County Meath but communications have changed even more, altering the 'practice' of medicine as I knew it in my early days in Summerhill. However, I must commend the calibre of young GPs with whom I worked in my later years, and I know I have left the care of my practice in Summerhill in very capable hands.

Ann McEntee

Man of Books

A native of Bohermeen, my working life was spent mainly in the library service in Meath, my father being from Martry and my mother being from Castlemartin.

My first school was the Mercy Convent, Navan. At that time boys went to either the Mercy or Loreto Convents before going on to the De La Salle Brothers. The Brother's school was located in an old military barracks on Abbey Road which was purchased by Dr Gaughran, Bishop of Meath. He had the building adapted for school purposes and in 1917 invited the De La Salle Brothers to run the school there.

For my secondary education I went to the Christian Brothers in Kells who ran both the primary and secondary schools there. One of the brothers in the primary school, Brother Murphy, promoted handball and was later to become President of the Handball Association of Ireland. He had experience of both the De La Salle and Christian Brothers and did not have any problems with either.

When I started work the library was located in what is now the Chamber of Commerce Building on Church Hill, Navan. It housed both the headquarters of the service and the Navan branch on the first floor.

The county librarian was Mrs M.K. McGurl who insisted on a policy of Irish being spoken by the staff when conversing with her and each other.

There was a network of branch libraries in the towns and library centres in schools and shops, post offices and private houses throughout the county.

After a number of years I was given charge of the distribution of books to the different branches and centres in the county. Branch libraries got a change of books once a year with smaller additions during the year. I had to travel to all the schools in the county twice a year.

Market Street, Kells.

Castle Street, Kells, showing the Cattle Fair in progress.

The service did not have its own transport and the distribution was by hired transport. One of these was Johnny Murray who had the contract for many years. Later Jimmy Smyth had the contract. Jimmy was a member of the Arcadians Showband and the father of Gloria (One Day at a Time). He had many interesting stories to tell of his days and nights on the road.

During that time I travelled, over a two year period, by bus to UCD two nights and two days a week to complete a Diploma in Library Training, which was essential, if one wished to gain promotion in the service.

After this I spent two years in Mullingar as an assistant librarian with the Longford Westmeath Joint Library Committee. At that time the two counties were combined for library services but today the service is run independently by both county councils. The town branch was in the Market House in the town centre and the headquarters in the old infirmary building on the Dublin Road.

It was operated by an independent board but was wound up in the 1930s when it was probably taken over by the council. From an old minutes book I saw that the last Chairman of the Board was a Fr Kennedy, a native of Cannon Row, Navan.

After a spell as county librarian in Mayo, where my work brought me into contact with a number of well known people including Padraic Flynn, Henry Kenny, father of the present leader of Fine Gael, and Eric Cross author of *The Tailor of Ansty*, I returned as county librarian for Longford, Westmeath where I spent an interesting five years.

In 1974 I was appointed county librarian for Meath. This was an honour and a privilege to be county librarian for my own county where I had started my career in the library service.

Over the years, when finances allowed, new and refurbished branch libraries were built in the county. The most interesting of these was the conversion of the old Catholic church in Dunshaughlin to a branch library. It was a challenge and the result was an attractive library in a unique building.

I always had a particular interest in the local s tudies section of the library. Over the years the collection was built up by purchasing material relating to the county from antiquarian and second hand booksellers. It was always with a certain amount of anticipation that catalogues were checked for items on County Meath.

Members of the public also donated material. One of these was Dr Beryl Moore who listed gravestone inscriptions in about 115 graveyards in the county. There is a complete set of these in the local studies section of the library.

The Meath Library Service also had a good relationship with the Meath Archaeological Society, members of which often brought local studies material to the attention of the library.

Local history requests were also interesting. One I remember from a lady in London who was compiling a list of White Horse Inns (Pubs) in Britain and Ireland. I gave her two that I knew of, one in Athboy (now gone) and one in Cootehill, County Cavan.

During my time in Meath I was involved with the Library Association of Ireland and had the honour of being President as well as serving as Hon. Secretary. I was also a member of An Chomhairle Leabharlanna, (The Library Service) and the Board of Trustees of the National Library.

Over the years many developments took place which changed the nature of the library service from being a books only service. The first of these was the large print books, which was followed by audio books and music tapes. Now of course the internet and CDs are a normal part of the service.

On a personal level I was always interested in sport and in particular Gaelic football which I played for many years. However, the sum total of my endeavour was a Minor Championship with Kilberry and a Junior Medal with Martry.

I also played badminton for many years and I remember playing in the old hall on the castle grounds just across the road from Trim Garda Station.

The library was an interesting place to work, as there was always an intake of new books, the product of man's, and indeed woman's, thoughts and ideas.

During my time as county librarian for Meath, the library had many visitors, two of whom I remember. One day there was a knock on my office door and a gentleman (unfortunately I forget his name) came in and said that there was someone to see me. It was the famous Irish author Peadar O'Donnell.

On another occasion we had a visit from Richard Boyle O'Reilly Hocking, the grandson of John Boyle O' Reilly.

Indeed I have to say that John Boyle O'Reilly is largely forgotten by the people of Meath and it was left to the people of Drogheda to promote interest in him and to arrange the annual commemoration in Dowth.

Liam Smith

Medical Memories

My first impression of Navan in the 1950s was of an unfriendly place. I was a blow-in, not a tourist. The impression was reinforced when an official of the Munster & Leinster Bank refused to cash the first pay-cheque from my employer, the Meath County Council. A shopkeeper obliged, thereby gaining a customer.

My days off were spent in Dublin with friends. Later, as I got to know the Meath people, Dublin lost its hold. The patients were a joy to look after and the staff was easy to work with. They seem in retrospect, like a big family.

On the ground floor were four medical wards, with the kitchen, pharmacy, Chapel and x-ray department and stores. There was no shop or restaurant. Upstairs were the surgical wards, theatre, children's ward, an office for clerical staff and a spare ward, which was used to accommodate an 'overflow'. The usual sluice rooms, bathrooms, etc. were at each end of the building towards the rear.

Behind this building was the Emergency, where stores were kept in wartime and soldiers came and went, I was told. It was transformed into a TB hospital, with huts in the grounds. TB patients were mostly young, cheerful and patient during the long illness. The Orthopaedic Hospital had not yet been built; the first Orthopaedic surgeon was Mr William de Wytt. It has filled a great need in the North Eastern Health Board area.

Facing the main hospital was a long building of similar style. It accommodated two house doctors, the nursing Sisters of Mercy, lay nurses and at one end the offices where Paddy ('put it in writing') Barry and his staff looked after overall administration.

The day-to-day running of the hospital was in the hands of the matron, Sister Michael, the antithesis of Hattie Jacques. She was succeeded by Sister Ignatius who could 'shoot from the hip', but was a born organiser and innovator.

Doctor Monahan was physician and surgeon to the entire hospital. He and his two house doctors did rounds daily, and were also on call. The house doctors worked long hours in the wards and were in charge of the pharmaceutical needs. Later a county surgeon was appointed.

Doctor Monahan had advanced ideas for the time, favouring raw vegetables and occasionally a Toxaemic Diet. The latter was a water diet, with tea, coffee and cigarettes cut out. It was usually prescribed for complaints, such as headaches, where there was no diagnosable cause. He had considerable psychological experience.

His house and farm, complete with cattle and horses, later became the site for St Patrick's School and a housing development.

Doctor Geraldine, Doctor Monahan's wife, was an eye specialist who had a large private practice and later attended patients in the clinic. Her brother, Frank Duff, co-founder of the Legion of Mary, is due for Beatification.

On the subject of religion, ministers of both churches attended the patients, performing Last Rites, etc. One old patient told Father Holloway that he did not need confession. 'There is no convenience here for committing sin.' 'Quite'.

In the 1950s, as today, there were the usual areas and cupboards for each ward. The medicine press contained liquid cures, pills, powders, aperients, etc. and also included what a patient called the 'Depth Charge' labelled 'Standard Mixture', the ingredients of which medical secrecy forbids me to divulge.

The poisons, Dettol, Lysol, Pot, Permanganate, lotions and soaps were separately stored, as were injection treatments, penicillin, streptomycin (then of comparatively recent use and of immense benefit) and paraldehyde, which was occasionally used for disturbed patients. Serum was kept in readiness for treating tetanus, which seemed to be peculiar in the area, Meath being a 'horsey' county.

The Fever (Infectious Diseases) Hospital was situated away from the other buildings and surrounded by a high wall. The nurses lived in a bungalow at the back, and worked and ate in the main building. I spent the greater part of my time nursing there, transferred without interview, unlike a friend who, being interviewed for a permanent post, had to translate from the Irish, 'Tá and gabhar ar mbohar, nil an gabhar ins an bpairc.' 'Whatever the escaped goat had to do with nursing.'

In the Fever, there were five nurses and we looked after a variety of cases. Patients with measles, whooping cough, scarlet fever, diphtheria, typhoid, meningitis, poliomyelitis and gastro-enteritis were treated. There had been an outbreak of polio in the area before I arrived. So frightened were the people of the town that when a fever nurse entered a shop, customers left hurriedly. At a time, five iron lungs were in use.

We had English patients from time to time from Butlins. They had incubated the diseases in Birmingham and Manchester.

Dr Galvin was the county Medical Officer. He called occasionally as did Dr Drumm before him.

In the grounds of the Fever Hospital was the 'Disinfection House' with a huge autoclave for sterilising mattresses, etc. No visitors were allowed.

The closing of the Fever hospitals was due in no small way to the excellence of our Public Health Administration and Management. We no longer have the outbreaks of infectious diseases of former years. Parents have co-operated admirably. Let us hope that this situation continues with the added responsibility of our increased population.

The grounds of Our Lady's Hospital looked very extensive before the car park. Orthopaedic and other ancillary buildings were established. There is an old graveyard where the 'paupers' who died were buried in the sad old days. There was a tennis court to the left as one drove in to the hospital. There were gardens with vegetables and even pigs for the swill. In true civil service manner, the gardener- groundsman kept a diary. Entered on one page was the sad announcement, 'One pig died today. I buried him.' There was a little petrol-driven cart in which turf was transported to the Fever for the ward fires, there being no central heating then. There were plenty of blankets and the seamstress made blue woollen jackets for the children. The equipment in the Fever Hospital included an iron lung, usual oxygen cylinders, and a respirator, steam kettle for the steam tent and a selection of drugs and applications. A jelly made from Carrageen Moss and milk was a favourite inclusion in Dr Monahan's diet and given to all babies. It and beef tea figured in the Typhoid diet.

Two very capable attendants and a cook completed the staff.

The old Fever hospital is now a very fine Ambulance Base. When I see the beautifully equipped ambulances now in use, I think of the plain transport vehicles of those days, (and for a time there was only one).

Each ambulance had two stretchers, kidney-trays or receivers for vomiting and a container for water which Paddy Carey, the driver, collected from the Lion's Mouth spring on the side of the road at Kentstown.

The suspension was not the best, so we jolted along the country roads. I'm sure the fine ambulances of today can negotiate the potholes of our modern roads with ease. Occasionally a patient needed to be transferred to a Dublin hospital, and on a hot day returning with an empty ambulance, Paddy was known to stop at Davy & Phelan's for a cool beer.

Sometimes patients had to be carried down fields where no ambulance could be driven, and as there was no second man one hoped that a good neighbour would help or a husband if the patient was a lady in labour on her way to Trim Maternity Hospital. With a late call and short labour, a traveller's baby sometimes en route. The ambulance man chewed his pencil, wondering what 'place of birth' he should put in the book.

Paddy lodged in a building called the 'Old Dispensary' beside the road to the hospital. He was succeeded by other drivers, all sterling characters. In fact, the same could be said of all the staff in the hospital, many of whom have gone to their reward, like some of those whom they cared for.

After the serious and sometimes stressful work on the wards we enjoyed a social life. There were two cinemas in the town. There were whist drives, badminton, yoga and pleasant areas for walking such as The Ramparts. There were tow dance halls for hops and 'dress dances'. We also danced at Trim, Oldcastle and Virginia and at carnival dances held in marquees elsewhere. Then there was Dublin, only thirty miles away.

We nurses, and the auxiliary staff had many a laugh. Our pay was laughable anyway.

Monica Sherlock

Above: Market Street, Trim, where two bookies operated opposite each other for most of the twentieth century.

Left: Ancient Cross, Kells.

Recalling the Past

The references here to such everyday tasks as making a potato pit and maintaining it and spraying the crop and thinning the turnips is bound to strike a nostalgic chord among those who can still remember what life was like in the countryside back in the 1940s and '50s.

This graphic account by Mary Seery of life then leaves little to the imagination and captures the atmosphere and mood of the age.

It's well I remember back in the 1940s how nothing was discarded mainly because most people were poor and there was a general awareness of 'waste not want not.' My mother taught me this valuable lesson which has remained with me throughout my entire life.

I'm thinking particularly of how almost every product from the farm was recycled to perform a different function. My mother was top class at this. I've seen worn coats sent to the dressmaker for turning inside out, and re-stitching. All types of handcrafts were the order of the day. I would like to tell you what I learned about spinning and part of how we lived on our Meath farm.

Spinning

Life was difficult and money was very scarce in most homes in the early 1940s (war years). Home industries, lace making, poultry rearing, vegetable production etc. were very much on the cards. It was my mother taught me how to spin. She used her spinning wheel to produce yarn, which was then used to knit socks, jumpers etc. or to provide finance to buy the necessary food stuffs.

When the shearing of sheep took place she secured a fleece, black or white from a local farmer. Depending on the variety of wool the price varied. £0.5s. Op would be the average price. The dirty pieces were removed from the fleece and the wool was dissected into small quantities as required. The portions for immediate use were oiled, teased out and special combs used to remove any remaining lumps, this process was called carding. It was then tolled softly in lengths of approx. 12", just large enough to handle. How often did I prepare a box full to have at the ready?

There were different types of wheel but the one we used was the one as illustrated. With a rhythmic movement using the foot pedal of the spinning wheel and simultaneously stringing out the wool to feed the shuttle, a single thread was created and mechanically wound around the shuttle until full. Using a second full shuttle, both threads were fed into the spinning wheel to make the final two ply product. Depending on the colour used one could achieve an all cream, all black, or what was known as a 'pepper and salt' effect by mixing the black and cream.

A special wooded frame was used on which the finished yarn was wound to form a hank and firmly tied at intervals. Remembering that it still contained oil which was applied at the preparation stage, it could now be washed and dried preferably outside, or knitted first and then washed to create a top class pure wool garment. There was demand for both washed and unwashed yarn on the local market.

General Farm Duties

Work on our farm was all labour intensive, as indeed it was everywhere else. My dad produced first class vegetables for table use, crispy fresh from the earth. Potatoes, cabbage, carrots, parsnips, peas etc. were grown for immediate use and the surplus pitted in the field for wintertime. My father made the pit with a first covering of straw and a second and third layer of clay pressed down and smoothed over without cracks. Branches were thrown over for protection. Sealing the pit properly was paramount. That was my father's territory and woe to the one who transgressed. Occasionally if my mother went short of a spud for dinner in his absence, whoever made the entry to the pit would be held accountable. Of course there was always an enemy, in this case the rat. Nature told him where the food was stored and by burrowing in he left a vent where the frost could penetrate resulting in disaster.

Attention to detail meant that food was preserved for the entire winter and beyond. Only potatoes were sprayed using 'bluestone' to prevent the dreaded blight. I can still taste those vegetables and the 'champion' spud.

As children we attended to many duties on the farm. Thinning turnips was a hateful job in the heat of the summer, not only had we our own crop to deal with but also our neighbours. The latter was needed revenue to secure groceries, etc. No precision sowing machines in those years. Going along the furrows, on our unprotected knees, leaving just one turnip to mature at intervals of approximately eight inches and attending to the weeds as we crawled along. I can still remember looking towards the headland aspiring to be there, another drill finished. We shuddered as the farmer arrived to check our work. The payment was small, nevertheless mother being the thrifty lady that she was, bought a baby calf for me from the farmer for, wait for it, £2. Delivered. Eventually he was sold for £14 and my first bicycle was secured. That was how we lived in those days, saving our pennies and putting them to good use.

In the 1940s when I was young, all the reaping and mowing was carried out primitively by the use of working horses. It took quite some time to complete a job. All day walking behind a plough or a mowing machine was an arduous task, to say the least, not to speak of the animals at the helm. Neighbours helped each other, lending machinery wherever it was required, no money exchanged, payment was the return of another similar deed. It was a humble way to live. From 1950 onwards change became rapid, more movement than had ever been seen before. It's good to document what life was really like. As my daughter said, we lived in a totally different world.

Mary C. Seery

Remembering Tullaghanstown Bog

While I was well aware that Kathleen Miggan was fairly accomplished at writing short stories and poems it was not until I interviewed her recently that I learned that she also an authority on things rural, particularly to do with the bog.

I would have been no more than ten years old then and being kept home from school would have been something that I looked forward to.

The preparations would begin the night before and with all the sandwiches and tea ready we would be up early the next day. A decision as to whether the turf was suitable to begin footing would be taken by one of the adults. After that it was up to the weather. No work would begin until the mist had cleared and we would have as many helping hands as possible. As children we would have many advantages, the most obvious being that we would be better suited to the stooping than the adults.

If the truth were told, we were not too keen on going to the bog and the least distraction was all that was need for us to take a break. So we took a keen interest in the insects and the birds and tried our best to raise a conversation on everything we came across.

As there was no such thing as a flask in those days we brought a kettle or two and lit a fire. This wouldn't happen today as fires are now banned from the bog. Between bouts of work we would have great fun jumping from bank to bank and maybe playing games such as clodding. Needless to say we would be in a fairly dirty state by the time the day ended but we could wash ourselves spotless in the bog water. Sometimes I would get the job of keeping an eye on the infants in their prams because our mothers brought the whole family to the bog, even the very youngest.

Our parents never brought a horse to the bog simply because the donkey was better for pulling the bog bogeys. These bogeys ran on rollers instead of wheels and were ideal for getting the turf out of the bog.

Footing entailed stacking the sods five high and we would try and build ours higher than anyone else, but anything over five high usually fell.

We would work hard if only for the reason that we would like to get away from the bog before the midges appeared and between these midges and the sunburn we would be fairly uncomfortable before the day was over. Then there was always one person, usually an elderly man, that would be finished before everyone else. His footings never fell and his bogey never got stuck. Our parents referred to him as the expert.

For all the hard work and sunburn and all the other discomforts I now look back to these days on the Tullaghanstown Bog as being among the happiest of my life.

Interview with Kathleen Miggan, May 2006

The Ancient Art of Thatching

Time was when one would spend most of their lives in just one occupation, trade or job. If one started out as a nurse or a postmistress or a doctor, then the chances are that that would be the only occupation that they would practice. The idea of being twenty years in one job was the 'in thing'.

If it had not been for the fact that many of the old skills became redundant it is safe to say that things would have remained like that indefinitely. Of course there are still plenty of people around who not only are still in the same trade that they started out in, but are actually carrying on where their fathers' left off.

Thatching is one trade that takes many years to perfect so that when one has eventually become proficient at it, it is highly unlikely that they would suddenly opt for another job. The thatcher is every bit as much a part of the rural scene today as it was a century ago.

Talking to Thomas O'Byrnes, I was struck by the depth of knowledge he has about this ancient art.

The late Tommie Farrell, flanked by farmers at Trim Market 1976.

It's something that I always loved doing ever since I was a youngster at home in Westmeath. I used to be fascinated with the way the elderly men used to thatch the cottages then. Later when I really became involved, I trained with a real expert, Peter Brockett, an Englishman down in Wexford.

I used to stay with the families that I would be thatching the house for. They would look after me and full board and lodging for the five weeks that it would take to do a full thatching job before I would move on to the next farmhouse. I suppose you could call me a sort of a journeyman. I got very hard to get out of Wexford.

Then when *Braveheart* came to Trim, I got the job thatching all the houses for the film. I also did thatching for J.B. Keane's film *Durango*. That was in Wicklow.

Anyway I'm now living in Navan and working on my own. At the moment I'm actually working on restoring a two hundred year old cottage at Moatlands opposite Our Lady's Hospital. It is a house that won an award in 1995 before being bought by a developer. The Meath County Council planning department however stipulated that it would have to be fully restored and it is this work that I am doing at the moment. The house had gone on fire and very little remained when I started work on it.

Is it a dying art? I asked Thomas.

Well up to the 1990s it was in decline but since that there has been an increase in the number of cottages being thatched in County Meath. The last of the old thatchers that I was involved with was a man called Jack O'Brien from Wilkinstown. He is dead now, God be good to him, but I learned a thing or two from him.

As well as thatching there is some coppicing going on at the moment especially in the Dunsany area. This is where the hazel rods and cut down to the stool and the quicks allowed to grow.

The new straw is much better now that the straw produced by the Combine harvester.

There is a family over in Ashbourne and they specialise in producing straw for thatching. It is cut in the old way with the reaper and binder and supplied to thatchers all over the county and indeed all over the country. It takes about five ton of straw to do the average house.

Interview with Thomas O'Byrnes on Saturday 28 January 2006.

five

Events

Bargaining for a pen of sheep.

Ballinabrackey and Castlejordan Gymkhana 1937

Just mention the word 'gymkhana' and I am immediately transported back to one of the first memories that I have of south Meath and particularly Trim.

This was the Trim Gymkhana and it was held in the 1930s in a field that used to be known as Connell's Field, located at the back of St Joseph's, or the County Home as it was known then. I remember the horses thundering down towards the winning post at the back of where Phil Cantwell and Peter Canning's houses now stand. It is one event in Trim that seems to have been completely forgotten about.

Gymkhanas were extremely popular in the years immediately before the war. I did manage however, to get some information on the Ballinabrackey and Castlejordan Gymkhana.

I was more than surprised when talking to some elderly people from that area some time ago and was told apparently they never heard of it.

Be that as it may, it appears that there were quite a lot of people involved in the event and it was a great day out for the people of the area. And one in which very little was left to chance as the page from the programme dated 12 August 1937 shows.

Even if it was only the stewards and the officials that turned out, not to mention the participants in the various events, a sizeable crowd would be assured.

With five races down for competition and a host of side-shows, all ages would be catered for. Between the first race, The Ballinabrackey Stakes would be underway by two p.m., to the final. Castlejordan Stakes would provide entertainment all the way with musical chairs, clay pigeon shooting and tug-o-war. Then of course the Ballinabrackey Fife and Drum Band would be in attendance with the usual selection of popular marches and all the latest numbers.

Bellewstown Races

Bellewstown Racecourse on the Hill of Crockafotha in County Meath is ideally situated in the rolling countryside in the eastern part of the county. The actual meeting itself is an annual three day event which takes place in the first week of July.

It is thought that racing first started at Bellewstown sometime in the early eighteenth century. English monarchs used to sponsor a race at Bellewstown right up until 1980 when the present monarch decided to discontinue the sponsorship.

Here Noel. E French, a noted local historian, tells the story of one of the most famous races ever to be associated with the course: the story of Barney Curley and Yellow Sam.

Barney Curley and Yellow Sam

Hello. Hello. Is that Uncle Pat?

How is she now?

Aw that's terrible when did she take the turn?

She was doing so well.

Shure, God is good.

Ya. Right you better go back. Put him on.

Your mother's doing a bit better today I hear

That's good news.

Hold on a minute.

Look! I'm on the phone, can you keep it down?

I'm in Bellewstown. The races are on – it's mad but sure it's better than being in a hospital bed.

Did they get the results of the tests?

It's the health service in this country.

Look my aunt is in the Lourdes in Drogheda and she is on her deathbed – will you give me a few minutes to talk to her family. If it was your mother who was dying wouldn't you want to be in contact?

What's wrong Seamus?

She has taken a turn for the worst.

Will you go away and stop bothering me!

What happened? And she was doing so well. Ya you had better put Sean on to me. You need to be holding her hand at a time like this.

Has she now? Ah there's life in the old bird yet.

Look, can't you see I'm on the phone?

The dying aunt went though a series of miraculous recoveries only to fall back on her bed, breathing her last gasp a few moments later.

And so it continued for the next thirty-seven minutes while the amateur riders' race went on outside the phone box. Nobody was going to interfere with a man who was talking to the family of his dying aunt. Well, would you? The next man in line to use the phone was a friend, colleague or should I say accomplice, of the chap on the phone.

The conversation, for the want of a better word, took place in 1975 in the days before computers, the days before the smoking ban, before mobile phones, in the days when it took the Department of Posts and Telegraphs two years and a half to install a phone in your home, and that was if you were lucky and knew a local TD who would put in a word for you.

The man on the phone, so concerned about his aunt, was on the only public phone in Bellewstown that day. In the last hour before the amateur riders' race at three fifteen, substantial amounts of money were placed in off-course bookmakers on Yellow Sam who was running in the race. All attempts to contact the bookies on the course to get the odds changed proved in vain as the only public phone in Bellewstown was in use. The on-course bookies never knew that there was a rush on the horse and the off- course bookies could not get through to have the odds changed, so Yellow Sam came good on the track at twenty to one, which were the odds which the off-course bookmakers had to pay on their bets.

Barney Curley, the celebrated gambler, and owner of Yellow Sam, had pulled off a major betting coup. Naming the horse after his father, Curley described Yellow Sam as one of the worst he had ever owned. Employing 125 people to put on bets all over the country, the bookmakers' suspicions were not aroused by the amounts being placed initially but realised that they had problems when they could not contact Bellewstown. A massive operation with meticulous timing, this perfectly legal coup netted a total of £370,000, well over two million in today's terms. The betting rules were changed to prevent something like it ever happening again.

The race took place on 25 June 1975 and twenty-five years later in the year 2000 the Bellewstown Committee held a race to commemorate the event with Barney Curley in attendance. This time he did not have to hide in the furze bushes to watch the racing.

And of course everybody was very sad for the poor bookmakers who lost all that money.

Noel E. French

Early School Days

Willie Hodgins is a native of County Meath, where in recent years he started to publish his work in the local press particularly The Meath Chronicle. *Here he tells us about his early school days.*

My name is William G Hodgins, (the G for George) and I was born on 19 August 1941, the third of William and Anna Hodgin's five children. We lived on a small farm at Faughan Hill, which is almost central to the four main towns of County Meath. Two months before my fifth birthday I began my education in Flower Hill School. This school was for Protestant children only and was situated on the north side of Navan town.

I can still remember my first day there; it was a very important milestone and the beginning of a lot of changes in my life. I had to rise at eight o' clock and after a hurried breakfast, walk a mile and a quarter to catch the bus at Tankardstown Crossroads, which is halfway between Kells and Navan on the main Dublin Road.

That bus was not run especially for the school children, but was the first bus of the day from Cavan to Dublin. Usually there were seven or eight other children, (all from a lot nearer the bus stop than I was) waiting to get on the bus when it came to a stop.

When we boarded we had to pay the conductor two old pence each for our passage. Sometimes there weren't enough vacant seats for all of us, so we would pack as many as possible on what seats were vacant and the rest would have to remain standing for the full length of the journey. When the bus arrived on the Market Square in Navan, we three, (Jim, Dolly and I) would have to walk another quarter of a mile to reach our school, while our RC counterparts had only a hundred yards or so to go to their school.

Although I had the company of both Jim, who was two and a half years older than me, and Dolly who was a year and a half older, my mother came along to help me settle in on that first morning. When she handed me over to Mrs McQuade the school teacher, I was put sitting beside a girl about my own age and we were both given sticks

Headfort Place, Kells in 1934.

Headfort House, Kells.

Above: John Street, Kells in 1920.

Right: Tommy Grimes.

of white chalk and slates to scribble on while she attended to her other classes. My new acquaintance and I soon got down to the business of making marks with the chalk on our slates and when a few minutes later I looked up from my work I could see no sign of mother; she having left for home when she saw me with my head down.

At the first lunch break I gave the teacher a small orange (one of three) I had in my little canvas school bag. This little offering, though well received at the time, brought me no favours with that 'Tree of Knowledge' because not many months later I began receiving my share of the punishment that she meted out to all miscreants and wrongdoers. Up to three hard slaps on the palms of each hand with her cane stick was what she had the habit of administering and it wasn't unusual for some unfortunate little reprobate to be at the receiving end twice or even three times in one day. Her cane never left her person but hung on her arm all through class, so it was always at the ready. Some days it seemed she was only delighted to get the opportunity to use it.

Yet for all her seemingly cruel ways she had a good-natured soul. Often when it happened that we were late for our bus in the evening, we tramped back to her house and she gave us bread and jam, with cups of well-sweetened tea to keep us going, while we waited 'till it was time to catch the next bus.

I was both tired and a little puzzled that first evening when I arrived home from school. Tired because of the long hard day and all the walking, and puzzled because there in front of my eyes when I opened my school bag, was the orange I had given the teacher. Later, as mother was getting me ready for bed, she asked me if I knew the girl's name that I had been sitting beside in school and when I told her, mother advised me to ask the girl to marry me when I 'd see her the next day. This I made sure to do; my very first proposal and the only one I have yet to receive a reply to.

I never got round to liking school. For me it was a place I had to waste too many hours, trying to learn how to do sums, speak the Irish language, spell correctly and obey the teacher. It would have been much nicer, I thought, if I was allowed to stay at home where I could follow my father around our few fields and help out whenever possible. But to school I had to go and to school I went every day, except when Jim decided that we would have a break. He always made sure to pick a morning when we were a bit late getting out of bed. Then as we rushed to catch our bus he would hold us back telling us all sorts of lies like; his foot was sore and he was unable to keep up or his braces were becoming undone and his trousers would drop if he quickened the pace. Before we got close to the bus stop he would suddenly halt, shade his eyes with his hand, look well ahead and say that he could see the bus pulling away, so we might as well go home.

These homecomings were not always welcomed. If mother was in the humour she would beat the delights out of both Jim and me with whatever was close to her hand, be it a sweeping brush, spade for lifting the ashes or whatever, while Dolly would get housework to do.

Sometimes, it seemed Dad was glad to see us arrive back, especially when we got a bit older and were able to help him. If it was planting time we would have to change quickly and either spread manure in drills or place the seed potatoes, (at equal spacing) on top of the manure that had already been spread. If it was the time for digging we would have to rush to the field with our buckets and help gather the spuds as soon as we had changed. These jobs though hard on the back were still a lot more attractive to Jim and me than schoolwork.

There were the odd times when mother almost welcomed us home. Days when dad was away working and she was running low on fuel. Instead of beating us she gave us something nice to eat and politely asked Jim if he thought he could manage to catch the donkey, borrow the neighbour's cart and go to the bog for a load of turf. He was always sure of two willing helpers at this job and in no time at all we would be heard singing our heads off as we trotted poor old Georgina (our donkey) to Bohermeen bog.

Life for the young was very simple in that early post-war period and even though there were few luxuries, parents seemed more willing than now to do without themselves so that they could give their children a good healthy upbringing. Looking back now I think that I was very lucky to be born and reared in that particular area of County Meath.

William G. Hodgins

It Happened on the Wettest Day Ever

On 8 December 1954, the wettest day Ireland has ever known, Mr Bill Connor and myself lodged some money in the Ulster Bank , Trim. This was the first money collected by the committee and members of the Scurlogstown Gaelic Football Club, of which I was appointed trustee along with Bill Connor.

Four years later in 1958 this club disbanded owing primarily to emigration and other factors. There was some money left in the funds and nobody had done anything about it, so on one sunny day in June 1968 I met Pat Farrelly and said, 'What will we do about that money which is in the bank belonging to the football club?'. He asked me what would I suggest and I suggested, 'pony racing'.

Pat Farrelly said, 'I will see Bill and a few of the lads and we will have a meeting'. Five of us, Bill Connor, Steve Connor, Pat Farrelly, Michael O'Neill and myself, met and at the meeting we decided to call in a week a further meeting to include the remaining members of the old Gaelic Club. At this further meeting the following officers and committee were appointed; Chairman, Tom Duffy; Vice-chairman, Michael Connolly; Secretary, Pat Farrelly; Treasurer, Bill Connor. Also on the committee were Stephen Connor, Norman Pratt, Felix McHugh, Jack Allen, Peter Fox, Pat Dunne, Michael Regan, P.R.O. Matthew Daly and Michael O'Neill.

At the meeting a lively discussion took place. First point discussed pony racing. When I offered a field for it, the point was settled quickly. The question then was raised, 'what is it in aid of?' When somebody suggested The Meath Handicapped Children it was agreed unanimously. Pat Farrelly then suggested some sort of entertainment in the Mill Yard. Frankly at the time I thought he was mad and could not imagine folk going in there to enjoy themselves. However, after some discussion it was agreed to. It was also agreed to inspect the premises when we had the permission of the owner, Mr Bernard McIvor.

Then the big question arose, 'what will we call the event?'

A long and lively debate during which many names were put forward and eventually Pat Farrelly came up with the title 'Scurlogstown Olympiad'. It was immediately adopted.

St Mary's church, Navan. The church is modelled on a Paris opera house. The opera house, which Father Eugene O'Reilly duplicated, was later destroyed by fire. Flawless acoustics and work by Edward Smyth, the famous eighteenth century sculptor who was born locally, are also notable features of St Mary's Church. A local craftsman, Christopher O'Brien, is credited with making two of the confession boxes for this church.

The next day we paid a visit to Bernard McIvor and his brother Charles. We were kindly received and permission to use the mill was quickly granted. To the gentlemen in question we owe a great debt of gratitude because without their good will and co-operation we could not have made a success of the Olympiad.

Next evening the committee visited the Mill Yard and anybody could see that nothing but an amount of hard work could have it ready for our fixed date, which was only six weeks away.

When the inspection was over Pat Farrelly asked me the question 'What do you think?' My reply was 'If the men are as good as they were in 1954 we will have it ready in time', because I knew from my experience with working with most of them they were not afraid of hard work and how right I was. From that moment on the ring of pick, the shovel, the spade, the saw, the axe, the thud of the hammer and the crunch of the tractor were heard in and around the mill often until two o'clock in the morning with nothing but good humour, laughter and some odd bursts of song. From all walks of life these men came. From the factories, the workshops, their offices and professions to help make the Olympiad a success. From the youngest boys and girls to the oldest man and woman each one played their part in full, but I feel sure there is one man whom I must single out for special mention and that is our secretary Pat Farrelly. If it were not for his courage, spirit and determination I think we would never have succeeded.

Then to every man and woman, boy and girl, and to everybody who helped in any way to make our Olympiad a success, my very sincere thanks. May God bless you and may you live long to enjoy the good work you have started.

The Ledwidge Museum and Cottage, Slane.

This piece, which was written by Tom Duffy who sadly is no longer with us, is reproduced here by kind permission of the Scurlogstown Olympiad Committee.

History will show that from these humble beginnings, the Scurlogstown Olympiad went on to become one of the most successful festivals in Ireland. Every year now during the summer the countryside as it was back in the 1940s and '50s is brought into town.

The highlight of the festival was and still is the Fair Day, or *Aonach Mor*, when the streets are literally taken over with farm animals, such as sheep, goats, pigs, fowl, horses, ponies, and other livestock. There are also displays and demonstrations from cobblers, blacksmiths, tin smiths, coopers and wheel wrights. Other trades and skills on display are sheep shearing, carding and spinning wool, arts and crafts, higglers, medicine men, politicians, fortune tellers and of course the street singer. Cheap John with his compliment of doubtful bargains always puts in an appearance.

In later years the festival became known as the Hay Making Festival. This idea gave the festival a much needed boost as young people that had never seen a mowing machine or a hay bogey at work looked on fascinated. It all happens in the shadow of some of the county's most spectacular ruins.

The aim of the Olympiad is to foster a love of our cultural heritage, the pastimes and the simple sports of our parents and grand parents.

An Aonach Mor on the streets of Trim

Scurlogstown Olympiad is a celebration of Ireland's cultural heritage and traditions. An Aonach Mor on the streets of Trim is an event nowadays held in the Porch Fields, a fifty acre site owned by Duchas and located on the banks of the Boyne overlooking Trim Castle. The Olympiad is billed as a National Haymaking Festival. All modern machinery is set aside, as the Meitheal gather with scythes, pitchforks and hay bogeys to save the winter fodder.

The children have great fun as they march behind the Wren Boys, or cuddle a new born lamb or bounce on the haycocks or spend a short time at the hedge school.

Pat Farrelly

Old Ways

The Rural Electrification scheme brought more than just light to the Meath countryside. It brought an end to a way of life that had existed for centuries, a come-up-to-the-fireside gathering that needed only that tap on the door.

Its attendant features would shift the focus away from the hearthstone to a box in the corner of the living room where people got their entertainment in prescribed doses, and it never really got dark anymore.

The world of a few generations earlier was a very different place. Night times gave over to the rosary or a neighbour dropping in, social chit-chat, intimate details bartered then as now, until the embers lent an other worldliness that was only a step away.

The coming of Christianity never banished the old ways, indeed in some ways it saved them. They were recorded and written down, finding their natural home now in text as well as in stories and storytelling, part of a tradition that saw no difference between man and his surroundings, where everything was a sign and a word could bring worlds into being.

Science throwing its own light on the subject dismissed them as so much superstition. A marrying of the mystical, with no truth in either, another piece of information and all would be explained, but one seemed to shadow the other, every answer bringing a new question in its wake. So now we look out on the universe and see only a small fraction of what is there, dark matter, very dark indeed.

The technological society of today seems very advanced compared to that of our grandfathers. Today villages throughout the county such as Summerhill, Kilmessan and Longwood shine with a brilliance that could never been imagined by the generation that went before us.

We have only to look around us today, no further in fact than to neon-lit shopping centres of Navan or Blanchardstown or Ashbourne, to see that our society is very advanced compared to that of our grandfather's time. Most of these benefits however were gleamed of insights of the nineteenth and early twentieth centuries and these in turn owed much to the framework laid down a century earlier.

The accepted view though was not one of concern to the ordinary person. The daily round and a landscape dotted with its reminders had its own truth. As one wit observed, when the electricity came on the lights went out. But then in one sense they had been going out for a long time, driven out by the famine and any number of wars. In the furniture factories of Navan the work went on oblivious of the new light that was beginning to filter through from the great world outside.

The emigrants that left the county in their thousands to build the great cities of England and America brought with them little more than their music and a number of stories handed down. Added to and embellished, they became an industry. Packed up with the bag and baggage, oil lamp and button box accordion we went from scooped out turnips to pumpkin heads, from All Souls to trick-or-treat until, if you pardon the expression, they came back to haunt us.

And so today we look back in wonder to this world of pookas and leprechauns and cures handed down, where every village from Nobber in the north to Ballinabrackey in the south had someone that could cure warts and whooping cough and every crossroads had a haunting.

People will still travel miles to see a faith healer. There are enough old cures in County Meath to merit a book. In every townland there is someone who knows someone that can cure some disease or other.

The realisation that we are governed by patterns would have been known but the marking of events was the turning point in more ways than one. The passage graves at Newgrange and other places throughout the county were aligned to the solar year and required a sophistication that was hard to credit. They have left us a wealth of knowledge that is still mostly unread and only half appreciated. The civilisation that grew up around the Boyne is said to predate the pyramids by perhaps two thousand years. Meath was even old then.

Frank Murphy

The Old School

When all the great events and adventures of our lives are long forgotten one event seems to stand out and that is the memory of our first days at school. I find it remarkable just how well even elderly people can remember the smallest details of their first day at the local school. People who have forgotten most of the other events of their lives seem to have no difficulty in remembering the lay out of the first classroom and the names of the teachers that might have greeted them sixty or seventy years earlier.

Going to school in the 1920s was very much different than it is today. Without the benefit of motorised transport and heated classrooms and indeed mobile phones, life for the school population would have been a fairly austere experience for all and even the rich had to do without most of the luxuries that today's school children take for granted. Maureen Murray went to school in the 1920s and here she recalls some of her memories of Johnstown (Navan) National School.

I went to Johnstown National School in the 1920s. The village of Johnstown at that time consisted of the school, a church, a teacher's residence and a small shop that sold sweets and buns. There is no trace of the school today, it having been demolished in the 1940s. There were two schools in the parish, the other one being in Walterstown about five miles away from Johnstown. At that time there were just two teachers and about sixty students but the numbers diminished during the '30s.

Some of the teachers that I remember were a Miss Hickey who was the principal.

Above left: John Spicer & Co. Ltd.

Above right: Tom Darby obliges with a tune on the button key accordion.

Market Square, Navan.

Then there was a Miss Gannon and a Miss Sexton. Like most national schools the inspector called every year.

The Parish Priest used to travel between the schools in a pony and trap.

Johnstown School, as far as I know, was built sometime in the 1800s and when I was going there in the 1920s it was a great big stone building, well ventilated and with a timber floor.

It had one fireplace in the centre and this was fuelled by coal and paid for by the parish. There would be a special collection every year to buy coal and this collection was also for the upkeep of the teacher's residence, which was across the road from the school.

We had little time to ourselves then and even our half hour lunch break was taken up with doing jobs such as gathering sprigs in Murphy's Wood near Kilcarne Bridge for the fire. The boys played football and the girls had their own games. I remember some of these games particularly: hopscotch, ring-a-roses and wallflowers and we had another game called statues. Between these games we would have to draw buckets of water from the pump across the road. This would be repeated when we got home in the evening because there was no water in any of the houses then.

Before we went on our summer holidays we had to clean every window in the school and scrub the floors so that the school would be spotless before we broke up.

I think that the teachers were strict because I remember one day when we were on our lunch break and the hunt came near the school. Fascinated by the spectacle, we watched the horses and hounds until well after the time was up. Then when we saw the teacher standing on top of the school wall with a cane in her hand we returned to the classroom only to get six on each hand for our little digression.

Interview with Maureen Murray on 18 January 2006

Whiskey Galore

My name is Kathleen Norris, formerly Kathleen Morgan, and I live on the Rós na Rí Road in Slane. I went to school in Slane National School and my teacher was Mrs Meade. I left school at the age of fourteen and went to work in a little grocery shop. After that I went to work in Slane Mills.

One of my most vivid memories of life in Slane, and particularly working in the mills, was of the night that lorry crashed into the bridge and into the Boyne. That was in April 1970 and over the years many lorries had crashed into this bridge but this one was different. I was actually at the weaving machine at the time; it was about seven p.m. when word reached the mill that a lorry had crashed into the bridge.

'What was it carrying?', someone asked.

'Whiskey,' came the reply.

One by one the machines were switched off as we made haste down to the bridge. Suddenly everyone seemed to forget about work, as the exodus became a stampede. After all, it wasn't every day that one gets the chance to grab a bottle or two of whiskey, and Bushmills at that.

Kathleen Norris

Academy Street, Navan.

Above: Academy Street, Navan as seen from the Railway Bridge. In 1802 the first Catholic school for boys, St Finians, was set up here. The college moved to Mullingar in 1908.

Left: 'Here's one you'll love'. Tom Darby plays another tune.

Left: Mosney, County Meath.

Below: This would have been a familiar sight to Andy Brennan as he marched through Navan.

six

Sport and
Leisure

Some of the most enduring names in the South Meath Battalion of the FCA, 1951. Rogers, Murray, Carroll, Clarke, Stapelton, McGew, Bell, Callaghan, Pierce and Cullen.

Promoting the FCA in the schools, Trim CBS Unit, 1954.

Syddan Remembered

Gaelic football has been played in Syddan as far back as the 1880s and '90s. By 1927 the club had won their first Junior Championship. Growing in strength they then went on to win the Féis Cup in 1932 and the Intermediate Championship nine years later in 1941.

Senior Championship victories followed in 1949, 1951, 1956, and again in 1952 when the club won the double of Féis Cup and championship.

In 1971 the club opened their new ground, Ludlow Park. The clubhouse was officially opened in 1995 when to mark the occasion there was a challenge match between Meath and Louth.

It was the Syddan Club in fact that presented the Keegan Cup to the county in honour of one of their players, Tom Keegan, who was killed playing for the club in the 1940s.

Trying to get information about this particular club would have been quite difficult if it was not for the fact that I happened to know one of the most dedicated supporters of the Syddan Club, Myles Clare. Myles now lives in south Meath and is a mine of information on not only his beloved Syddan but on Gaelic football in general.

I have always been a dedicated supporter of the Syddan Club and actually lined out for the successful team that won the Senior Championship in 1956. That was against Skryne and I was the youngest player on the team that day, if not actually on the field. Actually I played for Syddan at all levels minor, junior and senior. I played inter- county minor and junior. Later on in the year I captained the Meath team against Wicklow in Kells. That was the National League. At that time the team that won the senior championship would supply the captain of the county team

Can you recall any of the great players for Syddan in those days? I asked Myles.

Well of course there was my next door neighbour Bill Halfpenny and the other one was the great Paddy Meegan. Anyone that can remember when Meath won their first All Ireland in 1949 will remember how Paddy Meegan went through and when his shot at the goal was saved the ball came to Halfpenny who scored. Another great player was Bill Dillon. He played over three decades. He was famous. I know that he played in 1918 and again in the 1920s and '30s. Then, and indeed since, there was always a Dillon on the Syddan team.

What about training? I asked Myles.

Well there was nothing very sophisticated about our training. Twenty or thirty of us would gather at the crossroads six nights a week and all we would do was spend the time kicking goals.

Interview with Myles Clare in February 2006

Talking about Cricket

It is hard to believe that cricket was once played widely across County Meath. Before hurling, and indeed football, became popular it was cricket that reigned supreme in the sporting life of the county.

From Dunsany, where no less a personage than Lord Dunsany himself was one of the chief promoters of the game, to the Boardsmill area where there were dozens of teams within a few mile of each other, cricket was the dominant sport.

Just as in Dunsany there was a field known as 'The Cricket Field', there was another field in the Scurlogstown area also know as 'The Cricket Field'.

Seeing that most of the action on the cricket fields of Meath took place in the early years of the twentieth century it would be extremely difficult to get anyone to talk about the sport at that time. So finding someone as well informed on the sport as Larry Daly was something of a breakthrough.

Talking to Larry Daly about cricket one can sense a certain nostalgic yearning for the time when the game was at its height in south Meath. This, according to the eighty-four year old hale and hearty farmer, was in the 1920s and '30s when there were dozens of teams competing in the south Meath area. I asked Larry if he could name any of these teams.

Well there was one at Tobertynan. They played their games and practised on Stackpool's lawn. Then we had Summerhill, they played at the back of Shaw's!

There was a team up at Warrenstown that had their home ground at Shaw's. That's a different Shaw's by the way'.

There was a great team at Ginnets and they played their home games in Kit Kelly's field. Trim of course had a team. They played at the back of where the Malthouse Pub is now. Then there was a team out at Freffans. As a matter of fact there is a field out there still called the Cricket Field. Lord Dunsany played at Freffans regularly. Moymet and Bellewstown and Dalystown and Roristown, Rainstown and Kilmer all had teams. The Roristown Eleven practised and played in Eiver's back lawn. Bellewstown played at Cottage Hill. Kilmer played at Montgomerie's. Our own team Kilmurray played on Mason's back lawn. Our star fast bowler was Mick Cassidy.

There were some very good players. My brother Paul who is no longer with us was an overhand bowler, while my other brother Paddy was an underhand bowler. Then there was a man named Goggins who turned out for Moymet and he was fairly good too. As for myself I was a fielder. As for the stewards well I think that Dan Carr from Dogstown was the most efficient umpire in the local game.

What I didn't learn from Larry Daly during our conversation about cricket was hardly worth knowing. I learned Larry Daly was the kingpin of the Kilmurray team involved in every activity connected with the club. How they would call at Martin's shop before a game where they would be sprinkled with holy water. 'It must have been great fun,' I suggested.

We had a half barrel of single porter at every game. I remember one time when an ass got in and what he didn't spill he drank but he must have drank more than he spilled because he took off across the fields at a gallop that would have done justice to a Derby winner.

There was great rivalry between the teams, especially between Roristown and Kilmurray, and I remember seeing the late Vincent Eivers being bowled out with the first ball.

South Meath Battalion after winning the Battalion Shoot in the early 1950s.

Most of the time we made our bats out of boards but then we started getting them from Christ Bird's Pawnshop in Dublin. Christy Bird was probably the best all-rounder in the game at that time he played for Bellewstown. Another great player was Pat Rafferty, a bowler of distinction.

In some circles cricket was considered a foreign game and one man I know was suspended for just looking at a cricket match from the road. That happened in north Kildare.

It all came to an end in the early 1940 when the game of hurling became popular.

Interview with Larry Daly on Tuesday 3 January 2006

The Athletic Scene in Kells

In a county such as Meath where Gaelic football has dominated the sporting scene for so long, one might easily be inclined to forget that track and field events have and indeed have always had a substantial number of followers.

Maedhbh Rogan now works with the County Meath Library Service but in the 1970s and '80s she was a keen competitor in athletic events, not only in her native Kells where she was a member of the local club, but further afield as well. Here is Maedhbh's story.

I suppose coming from a family that was so heavily involved in athletics I would have a special affection for track and field events. I was born in Kells in 1969 and as

Navan around Andy Brennan's time.

Ludlow Street in 1951.

South Meath Battalion FCA, August 1951.

Boyne Area, Gormanstown Camp, 1951.

soon as I was able to get about I found myself running and generally taking part in competitions of that sort. We were a very competitive family and athletics provided a great outlet for our competitiveness. Added to this is the fact that both my father and mother saw to it that their offspring all seven of us were in a constant state readiness for every upcoming event.

My father Peter Rogan was an accomplished athlete in his day, having run in several marathons including Dublin and Belfast. (He now confines himself to walking marathons.)

My younger sister Aileen was probably the most successful in the family. She actually represented Ireland at events in Truro in Cornwall and in Belgium. My own greatest achievement was when I won the Leinster eight hundred yards under-twelve finals.

Then we used to take part in the Community Games in Mosney and one of the things we didn't like about this particular event was that while other counties got to stay there, the athletes of Meath had to drive there. This was I suppose on account of Meath's proximity to Mosney. Then there was the big cross-country event at Punchestown and another popular one was at Tullamore. Probably the most gruelling run that I ever had to endure was running a half-marathon in Connemara. That was a killer. We went everywhere by minibus and mother would pile in the whole family, all nine of us. She had the extra task of feeding us but her main job was getting us to the line in time and indeed making sure that none of us were left behind.

We weren't alone in Kells athletic circles at that time because there were other families equally enthusiastic about the track and field events. The Fitzgerald's and the Brady's and the Butler's were all into it in a big way.

We had other interests of course and one that I have good memories of was taking part in the Scór competition for dancing. Here again it was everyone in to the car or minibus and more travelling. That did involve a lot of travelling around the local halls. One venue that immediately springs to mind is The Lodge in Fyanstown.

This all happened during the late '70s and late '80s. After that there were other and more important considerations to be pursued and we had to concentrate in getting a good Leaving Cert and furthering our education.

Maedhbh Rogan

The Sunday Game

One of the great facts of life in rural Ireland down the years was the 'Sunday Game'. Sunday after Sunday, at dozens of playing fields across County Meath, the hurlers and footballers of nearly every parish in the county battled it out before spectators who lived for these encounters.

In football it was invariably teams from the strongholds of the game such as Navan, Screen, Walterstown, Syddan, Drumbaragh or Summerhill that would provide the action while teams from places like Trim, Kilmessan, Kildalkey, Athboy, Killyon or Longwood that would be in the spotlight.

Thus it was back in the 1930s when the game of hurling was in the ascendancy and thus it is today in these football years.

Growing up in County Meath one could be forgiven holding the view that there was in fact only one sport and that was Gaelic football. Indeed the road to Croke Park was one that was more familiar to Meath sportsmen and women than any other road in the country. With a string of successes going back to the 1940s and extending right down the years to the present day, it was hardly surprising that the youth of the county would be so keen to take the game of Gaelic football to their hearts. That other great game and one that Meath were so successful in back in the 1920s and '30s was always played under the shadow of the more popular sport.

Commenting on this situation, All Ireland Winning Football Captain in 1967 Peter Darby said,

'I do know that the game of hurling was somewhat neglected in favour of football and at a time when given half a chance the Meath hurlers could give some of the best teams in the country a run for it.'

Another Meath footballer, and this time from 1987 and 1988, Frank Foley had something to say on this subject too,

'I would say that even at the present time the strength of football in the county is preventing the game of hurling from taking off. Added to this is the fact that when football is strong in the county managers of clubs would want the young players to play the game which is stronger.'

Indeed not only has the strength of Gaelic football in County Meath had a detrimental effect on its sister game, but it has also kept other sports such as athletics in its shadow.

seven

Country Lore

Country Lore

Unexplainable happenings including sightings of the banshee have always played a part in the country lore of County Meath.

In 1968 Mrs Kathleen Lynch, who sadly is no longer with us, was walking home from the town of Trim to her home in Laracor. The evening, according to Mrs Lynch, was bright and there was a strong wind blowing.

We were approaching the Lough 'O' Biody Bridge, myself and my friend, when we were astonished to see a lighted candle burning on the jagged wall of the bridge, the naked flame apparently unaffected by the strong breeze.

In the twenty odd years between this incident and the disappearance of the bridge, sometime around 1980, there have been no further sightings of this unusual apparition.

For a description of the banshee we have to go to Bibi White, a Kildare woman living in Meath. Bibi told me she had had three sightings of the banshee, when I spoke to her during a Creative Writing class in Navan in 2005.

The first time that I saw the banshee was when I was eleven years old and that was near Kentstown, Navan.

It was a winter's evening when I saw the apparition in the form of a witch woman, no more than two feet tall. The strange creature walked around the farmyard three times before disappearing into the nearby graveyard. A few days later my uncle Paddy died. She appeared to me again the following year and again in 1957.

No one at that time thought that Bibi's story was unusual because it was generally accepted that the banshee followed certain families.

We have already seen what Meath Poet James Clarence Mangan had to say about the banshee. He also said that of the Meath families, the Kelly's would be the most favoured by the attentions of the banshee. Well another Meath poet who might have believed in the diminutive lady was Francis Ledwidge. In Alice Curtayne's book on Ledwidge, I came across the following sentence,

'He lived for his friends like Mattie McGoona who saw his ghost in Navan on the night of his death.'

Ledwidge himself mentions the banshee's wail in his poem 'Caoine' while in another of his poems 'A Life Lesson' he speaks of the Lanawn Shee, a spirit said to follow poets around.

Cottage at Moatlands, Navan, before it was destroyed by fire.

Above left: Bog Borrows in action, Tullaghanstown Bog, 1940s.
Above right: Thatcher George Kelly with two attendants, and of course Lassie the dog at Teach Scurlog near Trim.

THE THATCHER.

Thatcher at work, Rathmoylion area.

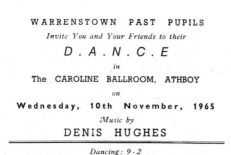

WARRENSTOWN PAST PUPILS

Invite You and Your Friends to their

D . A . N . C . E

in

The CAROLINE BALLROOM, ATHBOY

on

Wednesday, 10th November, 1965

Music by

DENIS HUGHES

Dancing : 9 - 2

Admission - - - - - 6/6

Garda Siochana   Navan District

GRAND DANCE

(In aid of Benevolent Fund)

IN BEECHMOUNT BALLROOM, NAVAN

FRIDAY, 19th OCTOBER, 1962

Dancing 9 to 2.

Music by DRIFTERS SHOWBAND

Admission .·. 6s.

BRIAN O'HIGGINS MEMORIAL

C O N C E R T

in

C.Y.M.S. HALL, NAVAN

on

FRIDAY, 28th MAY, 1965

ARTISTS :

GAEL LINN CABARET, First visit to Meath
MAEVE MULVANNY, of TV Ballad Fame
BRIAN O'HIGGINS, Abbey Actor
EAMONN KEANE, of Radio and TV Fame,
and a host of other artists.

Booking :

Fitzpatrick's Trimgate St, Navan

PHONE : NAVAN 36

COMMENCING : 8.30 P.M.

ADMISSION : 5/- (Bookable) 3/- & 2/-

NORTHERN AID (Athboy Branch)

Ceilidhe & Old-Time

IN RATHCAIRN COMMUNITY CENTRE

on Sunday Night, 26th September, 1976

Dancing 10 - 2   Music by CEOLTAS CEOLTOIRI

Admission - - - 60p

Tara Press Trim

Plenty of places for Monica Sherlock and her fellow nurses to go to during their time off.

110

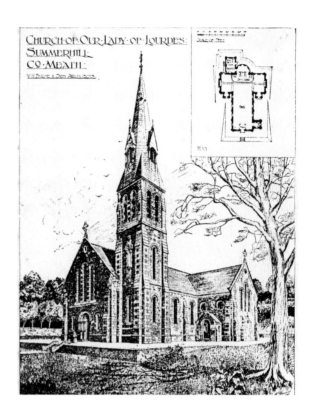

Right: Church of Our Lady of Lourdes, Summerhill.

Below: My mother, Mary Doggett of Grangegeeth, Slane (left) representing Meath at the All Ieland Spinning Demonstration in the RDS Dublin in 1946. Lady on the right is unknown.

Picturesque Bellewstown where the lengthening shadows suggest an evening meeting at the famous east Meath course.

Another famous east Meath course, racing on Laytown's golden stand.

A hilarious story

One of the first images that appear to the traveller entering Meath from the Dublin direction is that of a man in the act of closing a gate and waving. It is an image, according to the creator of the sculpture, that is repeated right across the county and reflects the county's preoccupation with gates.

Up to quite recently there was a gate on the Navan Road out of Trim that had, according to local tradition never been seen closed. It was known as Niblock's Gate and Matt Gilsenan tells this story about it that borders on the hilarious.

Well apparently one night a group of local men decided to close the gates. After doing just that they hung around for a while to see if the gates would open by themselves. Eventually satisfied that the gates were firmly shut they headed for home.

However, the next morning at breakfast one of them was terrified to learn that there had been a fatal accident at the spot. It happened, he was told, when the postman went riding up to the gates and expecting them to be open he rode slap bang into them with fatal consequences.

Apparently someone had got wind of the attempt to close the gates and had concocted the story about the postman.

Strange Happenings

Born and reared in the Dunderry area of south Meath, John Darcy went to school in nearby Trim and finished his education in Roscrea College. A keen historian with a flair for the written word John, who is now a patient in St Colmcille's Nursing Home in Kells, comes from one of the oldest and most respected families in Meath. The family have actually been in Dunderry since the early nineteenth century. Before coming to Dunderry the Darcy family lived in the famous Dunmoe Castle, one of John's ancestors having the title of 'The Lord of Dunmoe'. At that time, according to John, the Darcy's owned all the land between Dunmoe and Slane. With such an interesting history it was only to be expected that John would have more than one story to tell.

He could have told stories about football or hurling or about his beloved farming but he chose instead to relate some of the folklore of his native Dunderry.

Oh, indeed there are some stories about gates in this area too, the most common being the one about the gates on the large house between the villages of Dunderry and Robinstown. The house itself was a big old barrack type building set on about three hundred acres of parkland. It was surrounded by huge old trees that gave the place an eerie atmosphere. Sometime in the early years of the twentieth century an elderly English couple occupied the house. This couple, the story goes, were somewhat eccentric. They employed a butler in addition to other servants and threw lavish parties. Local people were well used to seeing the gentry arrive and depart in all their finery.

One story told about this house concerns a temporary servant and his girlfriend that were hired to look after the place when the owners were away. One evening when they were walking down the avenue the big gates suddenly swung open to allow them through. Once they had gone through the gates slammed shut.

Pat Seery mowing the meadow in the early 1940s.

Above: Haymaking in Meath.

Opposite above: Summerhill Post Office.

Opposite below: Dangan Castle, the birthplace of the Duke of Wellington in the parish of Summerhill.

St Patrick's Day Parade in Trim's Patrick Street.

Above: Between the Yellow Steeple and the Sheep Gate overlooking the Boyne, this is the site of the annual Scurlogstown Olympiad.

Opposite below left: Mattie Lynch, former postman for Rathfeigh making a presentation to Kay Halligan on the occasion of her retirement as postmistress of Rathfeigh Post Office.

Opposite below right: St Patrick's church, Trim in 1925.

Above: Despite its unstable appearance, this ancient bridge over the Skane River at Killeen continues to carry most of the traffice between Kilmessan and Dunshaughlin areas of County Meath.

Another incident connected with this house happened when one of the servants was on his way home from Bective Mill on his horse and cart. For no apparent reason he suddenly began to sweat and felt that there was somebody behind him. When he did look around he saw a large wool pack rolling after him. It rolled right up behind the cart and followed it until it reached the bridge when it disappeared. Sadly the man died that very night.

While the mystery of the stray sod is not peculiar to County Meath it, according to John Darcy, was fairly established in the Dunderry area. Somewhere in the vast acreage of land that surrounds the village there is at least one field that contains a stray sod. It was here in this field sometime around 1970 that a group of men were engaged in clearing some blackthorn bushes and furze to make way for crops.

Having finished the day's work they made their way to the farmyard and were suddenly surprised to find that one of their number was not with them.

It was getting on for twilight and one could understand their anxiety as they toyed with the idea of going back to find him. After discussing the situation they eventually decided to go back to the field and see could they find him.

One can imagine their surprise when they arrived at the field and found their fellow worker walking round and round in a small circle in the centre of the field. He seemed to be in some kind of trance and was completely unaware of their presence. Grabbing him by the shoulder they eventually led him to the safety of the farmyard where after a cup of tea he proceeded to tell them of his experience.

Apparently he had stepped on a stray sod and try as he might he couldn't find his way out of the field. At first he had searched around the edge of the field looking for the gate, but unable to locate it he had kept going around in ever diminishing circles until he eventually found that he was walking round and round in the centre of the field, just as they had found him.

Interview with John Darcy in St Columcille's Nursing Home Kells,
9 January 2006.

The Lone Bush

Travellers going through parts of the midlands including County Meath have often commented on the frequency of lone bushes in the middle of cultivated fields. Most however, would have been unaware of the legend attached to these bushes. Further evidence of the legacy of the lone bush has come to light from time to time and in various locations throughout the county. Road works and other civic projects have actually been held up because it was not possible to get local workers to cut them down. This often resulted in foreign labour being enlisted to do the work which local workers would have nothing to do with.

An article in the 'Meath Chronicle' as far back as 1931 carried the headline, 'The Lone Bush At Oldcastle', with the sub-heading 'Removed by Contractors—Foreboding by Elders'.

The report tells of the experience of an employee of Messers A. Doyle and Sons, Contractors Kells who were building a house for the Meath Health Board.

It appears that a notice board was being erected on the site and, in the course of the process of the work, a bush which was in the way was removed. Now this was no ordinary bush. It was actually known as the Lone Bush around which the fairies were supposed to congregate. Some of the older men in the area were not happy about the cutting down of the bush and they shook their heads forebodingly.

Frank Murphy poses on Bellinter bridge across the River Boyne.

Pat Farrelly leads the Scurlogstown Olympiad contingent through the streets of Trim for the 1992 St Patrick's Day Parade.

The Show in the Porch Fields, the other big agricultural event of the year.

An ivy-clad St John's Castle near Scurlogstown, Trim.

Slane with its bridges and Weirs as it appeared in the early twentieth century.

The Boyne at Trim 1928.

Running boards and bumpers, High Street, Trim in the 1950s.

Market Square, Navan. Willie Hodgins would still have a quarter of a mile to go to school from here.

Larry Daly, star fielder with Kilmurray Cricket Team.

Nellie Kane's Cottage, Laracor Road out from Trim, is one of the few thatched cottages in the area.

The Meath football team, courtesy of *The Meath Chronicle*.

Parish Social

IN KILDALKEY HALL

on Friday 6th January '84

Music by★ THE SUPERTONES

Dancing from 10.30

Tickets - - - - £2

Tara Press, Trim

Kildalkey Hurling Club   №   0

Annual

Three Fifteens

IN KILDALKEY HALL

ON SUNDAY, 20th NOVEMBER, 1977

AT 9 P.M. SHARP

IN PRIZES **£100** IN PRIZES

Tickets   (including supper)   £1

Promoter

Tara Press Trim

KILDALKEY HURLING & FOOTBALL CLUB

DINNER - SOCIAL
&
PRESENTATION OF MEDALS

in the

CASTLE BALLROOM, TRIM

on

FRIDAY, 12th NOVEMBER, 1971

Dinner 9.30 p.m.   Music by Mexican Trio

TICKETS - - - - £1.50 Each

Tickets should be obtained before Monday, 8th November, 1971

Kildalkey Badminton Club

The Committee of above invite you and your friends to their

★ D·A·N·C·E ★

in DELVIN HALL

on SUNDAY, 24th APRIL, 1966

MUSIC BY THE FABULOUS......

CANADIANS SHOWBAND

DANCING FROM 9 P.M.

Admission 6/-

The social scene in Kildalkey in the 1960 and '70s.

Above left: A youthful Bibi White in 1954.

Above right: Ballinabrackey and Castlejordan Gymkhana.

John Treacy (second from left), Maedhbh Rogan (wearing No. 2). Community games, Mosney, September 1981. Pictured after Maedhbh had won the heat of the under twelve's 600 metres.

Be that as it may, according to the report one evening this week a workman was going back to the site for some purpose, and standing where the Lone Bush used to be was a fairy. The incident caused considerable interest in the town, where many similar incidents were recalled by the older people.

The Unexplainable

Finding people that are prepared to talk openly about unexplainable happenings is understandably difficult.

The fear of not being believed or being laughed at would be the main reason for this. Yet for all that it is safe to say that very few people go through life without at least one or two encounters with the unexplainable.

Country lore in County Meath is reflected in the dozens of old castles, old mansions, stately homes and of course humble cottages, that have over the years become associated with the afterlife. In the matter of folklore it would appear that Meath had a head start on the other counties with names such as Tara and Newgrange continuing to evoke curiosity.

For the most part the vast majority of these mysteries are explainable or at least grossly exaggerated. Yet we will lose something if we ever lose our folklore.

Whether Meath is unique in this respect it is difficult to say, except that in some areas the rules laid down for the royal county are different to those of other counties.

Almost every house built in Meath today would have to conform to certain planning conditions. Stipulations however, dictated by centuries of folklore and superstition, might not always have been adhered to. This would have resulted in the wrath of the spirits descending on the offender.

In some counties for example it was considered unlucky to build an extra room on the north side of the house while in other counties it was the south side that was considered unlucky. Building a replacement house directly across the road from the existing house was strictly taboo in some counties.

In Meath we had our own superstitions when it came to house building. Up to fairly recently it was considered extremely unlucky, indeed fatal to raise the roof or build an extra storey on an existing house.

Every county it would appear had its own superstitions and our own county of Meath was no exception.

A Case of Mistaken Identity

I have this observation from Martin Faulkner, a member of the Irish Wheelchair Association, from Slane.

You're driving along in your car, when you see someone you know, you wave to them but on coming nearer to them you discover that you were mistaken. It was in fact someone else that you waved to.

Not to worry. Nine times out of ten the person that you thought that you recognised will be the next person that you meet. Apparently it also happens when you are walking along the street or road as the case may be.

Whether this is peculiar to County Meath or not I am not quite sure, suffice to say that this was

Very little doubt as to what county these old timers were lining out for.

something that I never heard of until the man from Slane pointed it out to me. So as far as I am concerned, it has its origins in County Meath.

Other Irish titles published by Nonsuch

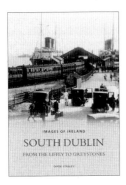

Images of Ireland: South Dublin
DR DEREK STANLEY

From the Liffey riverside to the picturesque coastal scenery, this book is a fascinating collection of old photographs and postcards that chart the past century of South Dublin history.

ISBN: 1-84588-566-X Price: Euro 16.99

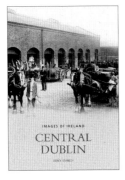

Images of Ireland: Central Dublin
DR DEREK STANLEY

Dublin is a vibrant and modern European capital city, with a long distinguished history dating back to the time of the Vikings. This book displays the immense character of the city centre through a striking collection of photographs and postcards.

ISBN: 1-84588-567-8 Price: Euro 16.99

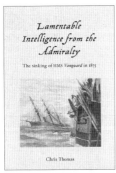

Lamentable Intelligence from the Admiralty
The sinking of HMS *Vanguard* in 1875
CHRIS THOMAS

HMS *Vanguard* sank in thick fog in Dublin Bay in 1875. The unjust verdict handed down by the Court Martial marked this incident as significant in naval history. This book revisits the sinking exploring the joys and trials of seagoing life in the Victorian era.

ISBN: 1-84588-544-9 Price: Euro 21.99

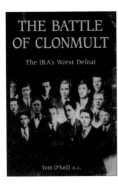

The Battle of Clonmult
TOM O'NEILL

The 1921 Battle of Clonmult is known as the IRA's worst defeat. This book provides an inight into the days preceding the battle and the progress of the battle itself. It is an invaluable guide to the history of the IRA in Cork.

1-84588-554-6 Price: Euro 12.99

If you are interested in purchasing other books published by Nonsuch, or in case you have difficulty finding any Nonsuch books in your local bookshop, you can also place orders directly through our website:

www.nonsuch-publishing.com